REVOLUTION IN CONNACHT

Members of the IRA, South Galway.

Courtesy of Finian Ó Fathaigh.

REVOLUTION IN CONNACHT

A PHOTOGRAPHIC HISTORY 1913–23

CORMAC Ó COMHRAÍ

MERCIER PRESS
Cork
www.mercierpress.ie

ISBN: 978 1 78117 132 5

10 9 8 7 6 5 4 3 2 1

A CIP record for this title is available from the British Library

Printed and bound in the EU.

CONTENTS

INTRODUCTION

The years 1913–23 saw an incredible series of events in Ireland and the term 'revolution' in the title of this book refers both to political revolution and to threats to the social order that arose as a result. The revolutionaries, often the young people, the poor people and women, defied, and even gained power over, those who were more powerful than they were. However limited, that was revolutionary.

It was ordinary people who were the backbone of the revolution in the west of Ireland, people like Patrick Glynn (*left*). Glynn was from the Kilbeacanty area of South Galway. Born in 1891 to a rural family, he would have experienced a strong sense of community growing up. In an age before mechanisation the help of neighbours was essential

to small farmers working the land, as this photograph of a group working on a bog in South Galway indicates, and that sense of community was later essential to the IRA's survival.

Glynn joined the Irish Volunteers in 1917 and fought the forces of the British and then the Irish government. He saw people die violently and must have imagined death, torture or his family becoming targets. Many of the men involved in the fight became lifelong friends, and it was through his involvement with the revolutionary movement that Glynn met his wife. The question of what people like Glynn felt, endured and inflicted on others is at the heart of this book.

Glynn's grandfather had also been involved in Republican politics and his father had been a land agitator. Republicans cherished historical family links with the United Irishmen, instigators of the 1798 rebellion, and the Fenians (Irish Republican Brotherhood), who rebelled in 1867. Tommy Wilson from Cortoon (G)[1] recalled hearing about a Fenian relative:

1 The letters in brackets throughout the book after people's names or places

> Instead of a prison sentence, he was sentenced to be scourged as an example to his colleagues in the Fenian Brotherhood. He was tied to the back of a horse cart in the Square in Tuam, stripped to the skin and whipped, from the Square to the bridge in Shop Street, a distance of over a hundred yards. At the bridge, he was untied and he remarked, 'Thank God! I'm none the worse of [*sic*] it.' ... For the remark, he was again tied to the back of the cart and whipped back to the Square.[2]

Folklore conditioned young people in the west of Ireland to be, at the very least, wary of the state. Many considered themselves to be part of a community wronged by that state. Glynn was raised during an era when Irish was being replaced by English in South Galway as the language used in child-rearing, but not for cultural expression or adult conversation. At social gatherings Glynn heard songs in both Irish and English and later commented: 'Through those songs I got my first lessons in Irish history and learned enough from them to realise something of the fight put up by my countrymen against the invader.'[3]

The language shift was welcomed by some, but resented by those who blamed the British, as well as the economic and education system, for the shift. Some linked Anglicisation with a modernisation that had seen the growth of urban squalor and a perceived decline in morality. A number of urban-based intellectuals began to try to promote Gaelic culture, hoping it would take its place among modern European cultures. In the photograph overleaf is the cast of an Irish-language play. The man with the violin is Douglas

---

indicate the county that they belong to. Thus (G) = Galway; (SO) = Sligo; (RN) = Roscommon; (LM) = Leitrim; (MO) = Mayo.

2 Thomas Wilson, Bureau of Military History (BMH) Witness Statement (WS) 1183, p. 1.

3 Patrick Glynn, BMH WS 1033, p. 1.

Hyde, a Frenchpark (RN) Protestant, one of the driving forces of the Gaelic revival and later the first president of Ireland.

The Gaelic revival made revolutionaries of some, but its impact never received the support its advocates or detractors claimed. Among the better off, only mavericks embraced it, such as Patrick Pearse, pictured on the next page in front of a crowd at a Gaelic League aeraíocht (cultural festival) at

Rosmuck (G) some time around 1905. Gaelic culture continued to be seen as a badge of the poor or the uncivilised. Ernie O'Malley, born into an upper middle-class family in Castlebar (MO), later wrote: 'when I was called Ó Máille, our name in Irish, I was insulted. That was not my name; only the poor used it. I would have none of it.'[4]

In Irish-speaking districts it was difficult for the revivalists to make inroads among people who saw preparation for emigration as an integral part of child-rearing. Membership numbers provide an indication of the limited nature of the revival's impact. In January 1919 it was reported by the police in Mayo that the county had 2,741 members of the Irish Transport and General Workers' Union, 3,966 members of the agrarian United Irish League and 6,613 members of Sinn Féin, but only 819 members of the GAA, which promoted Gaelic games, and 649 members of the Gaelic League, which promoted the Irish language.[5]

4 E. O'Malley, *On Another Man's Wound* (Cork, 2013), p. 19.

5 D. Price, *The Flame and the Candle: War in Mayo 1919–1924* (Cork, 2012), p. 17.

The fight to preserve Ireland's heritage was not the only one going on in the late nineteenth and early twentieth centuries. Pat Glynn would have seen extensive poverty. In 1917 in Mayo, for example, there were 17,000 farm holdings under fifteen acres.[6] The desire to acquire land was at fever pitch and he would have witnessed a shift in the focus of the land agitation movement during his youth. The landlords' power was waning and their land was being transferred to the general population as the British government responded to communal agitation with a programme of loans and incentives to facilitate this. Despite that, memories of evictions remained fresh, such as the one in Woodford (G) pictured below, and some Republicans had even witnessed such events.

With the transfer of the land underway, the land agitators' major enemies were now the cattle graziers who sought to maximise profits by creating ranches. This set them at odds with those who believed that land should be distributed in such a way as to increase the amount of families who could live comfortably on it. Some of the graziers were former landlords who had

6 C. Breathnach, *The Congested Districts Board of Ireland, 1891–1923* (Dublin 2005), p. 159.

retained parts of their estates, some were urban shopkeepers, some investors. Moderate and radical nationalists exploited the land question to gain support by encouraging agitation and defiance of the rule of law, but it was never fully clear whether they were controlling the campaign or it was controlling them. The Ranch War was a largely Connacht-based communal revolt, which spread into the midlands and Clare in the early twentieth century. Cattle drives scattered the grazier's herds and, when rounded up, these were promptly re-dispersed at the first opportunity. John Stenson, the only fatality of the 'war', was shot dead in Riverstown (SO) when the Royal Irish Constabulary (RIC) fired on a crowd driving cattle.[7] Pictured above is Clonbrock House (G), which was the subject of a vigorous campaign for land division during this period.

Before, during and after the Ranch War, agrarian violence was common, much of it carried out by the local members of the Irish Republican Brotherhood (IRB), a secret revolutionary group dedicated to freeing Ireland from British rule through insurrection. Agrarian agitation brought communities into conflict with the RIC, rural Ireland's armed police force. Areas where

7 F. Campbell, *Land and Revolution: Nationalist Politics in the West of Ireland 1891–1921* (Oxford, 2005), p. 174.

there was a tradition of land agitation saw large numbers of RIC men posted to them, such as Oranmore (G) where the men below were based. In the centre, standing, is Constable Thomas Browne, who was stationed in Oranmore throughout the War of Independence (see also p. 79).

Despite the complaints of bias and violence made by Republicans and land agitators against the police, RIC men were generally respected and policed their communities well during settled times. One Moycullen (G) Republican remembered the difficulty they had in convincing people to turn against the local RIC sergeant: 'B'fhearr céad uair corp rógaire mar b'fhusa an pobal a shéideadh ina aghaidh.' ('You were better off with an absolute rogue because it was easier to turn the community against him.')[8]

The typical RIC constable/sergeant throughout the country was a Catholic and usually the son of an RIC man or a small farmer from the western seaboard. One such man was Michael Guilfoyle (*right*), who came from an RIC family – his father and brother also served. Born in Enniscrone, Sligo, he was a sergeant in Belmullet (MO) when the force was disbanded in 1922.

There were a number of other key issues in the run-up to the years of revolution. Sectarianism was much less significant than it had been in previous generations, but religious tensions could become a factor when mixed with other grievances such as land, education, employment and missionary work. Except in urban areas and pockets of Sligo and Leitrim, Protestantism was weak in Connacht and declining, demographically speaking. There were a number of reasons for this: the population was dispersed and they were predisposed to migration as many had been born elsewhere and worked either for the state or the 'Big House'. They did, however, continue to supply a large proportion of those involved in supplying essential services to the community, such as banking or medicine.

Unionists or loyalists, who favoured being ruled completely from Britain, formed a tiny minority of the population in Connacht and were largely Protestant. The vast majority of the population were nationalists who wanted a parliament in Dublin. Their

8 T. Bairéad, *Gan Baisteadh* (Baile Átha Cliath, 1972), p. 103.

party, the Irish Parliamentary Party (IPP), dominated politics: it won both Sligo parliamentary constituencies without contest from 1895 to 1918.[9] A number of the IPP's western leaders had spent time in jail as a result of their involvement in agrarian agitation, including John Dillon, MP for East Mayo, pictured above (*seated, left*) with a group of supporters in Athlone. As well as the agrarian United Irish League, the Catholic Church and a Catholic fraternal organisation, the Ancient Order of Hibernians (resented by Republicans for its sectarianism and conservatism) were the IPP's allies. The IPP's main policy was to try to achieve limited independence known as Home Rule by working within the British parliament, something that more revolutionary nationalists felt did not go far enough. Tension grew between small nationalist parties, such as Sinn Féin, and the supporters of the IPP, and difficulties in maintaining nationalist unity sometimes resulted in intimidation and even violence against

9 M. Farry, *Sligo 1914–1921: A Chronicle of Conflict* (Trim, 1992).

dissident nationalists. By late 1912 it seemed Home Rule would become a reality, and the reaction to this by Unionists would push Ireland towards a more radical and violent future.

Image of Patrick Glynn courtesy of the Stanford and Glynn families; image of group working in bog courtesy of John Reilly; image of cast of an Irish play courtesy of Kilmainham Gaol Museum, 12PC-1A25-02; image of Patrick Pearse at Rosmuck courtesy of the Pearse Museum; image of eviction courtesy of the National Library of Ireland L-Roy-02482; image of Clonbrock House courtesy of the National Library of Ireland Clon_464; image of RIC courtesy of Paul Browne; image of Michael Guilfoyle courtesy of Michael Guilfoyle; image of John Dillon and supporters courtesy of Athlone Library.

FROM HOME RULE TO A REPUBLIC: 1913-18

I thanked God for seeing such a day.
Tom Maguire of Cross (MO) referring
to the news of the Easter Rising.[1]

By late 1912, when it finally seemed that Home Rule would become a reality in Ireland, nationalist Ireland rejoiced, but Unionists in Ulster did not. Fearing the power of the Catholic Church, land agitators, a vengeful or sectarian nationalist population and the severing of ties with the British economy, they formed the Ulster Volunteer Force (UVF) and threatened armed rebellion if partition was not introduced. In response nationalists began to organise themselves to protect thirty-two-county Home Rule. An attempt was made in Athlone to create a pro-Home Rule paramilitary force called the Midland Volunteer Force, which then became part of the Irish Volunteers, founded in Dublin in November 1913. By the end of the year the Volunteers were spreading rapidly all over the country. Pictured are members of either the Midland Volunteer Force or the Irish Volunteers drilling in Athlone.

Courtesy of Athlone Library.

1 J. Augusteijn, *From Public Defiance to Guerrilla Warfare* (Dublin, 1996), p. 60.

The Irish Volunteers relied on ex-British soldiers for their training, and Colonel Maurice Moore (*above*), a landed Catholic from Moore Hall (MO) and a Gaelic enthusiast with extensive British Army service, became Inspector General of the Volunteers, inspecting units of the Volunteers to ensure their efficiency.[1] Afraid of the outbreak of civil war and unsure of whether or not the British Army could be relied upon to impose its will, the British government started to prepare for partition. Ultimately it was the First World War that began in 1914, rather than government policy, which prevented civil war.

Courtesy of Mercier Archives.

1 Price, *The Flame and the Candle*, pp. 20–1.

The leader of the IPP, John Redmond, and his party actively supported British Army recruitment for the war. This is reflected in propaganda from the time, such as the poster seen here. The vast majority of nationalists agreed with this policy, but the more radical nationalists felt that the Volunteers should only be fighting for Ireland's freedom. This led to a split in the Volunteers, with those loyal to Redmond and the IPP forming the National Volunteers and the dissidents retaining the name Irish Volunteers. The latter comprised a tiny minority and increasingly came to be called

'Sinn Féiners', after the more radical political party, to distinguish them from those who supported the IPP's stance. As the war dragged on and became increasingly unpopular, the identification of the IPP with recruitment damaged the party.

Courtesy of the National Library of Ireland, EPH 113.

Opposed by all the powerful forces within Irish society – the IPP, the Church, the establishment, the media and business – by the start of the twentieth century the IRB had waned in influence and support in many areas. It was then revived in the first decade of the new century by a younger generation of Republicans, not least Seán Mac Diarmada, a Kiltyclogher (LM) man. Mac Diarmada was completely dedicated to the cause of Irish freedom, even describing his religion in the 1911 census as *náisiúntacht na hÉireann*, meaning Irish nationality, and he would be executed for his part in the 1916 Rising.[1] The IRB gained control of the Irish Volunteers after the start of the First World War by secretly infiltrating the organisation, and, with Britain preoccupied by war, began to plan for a rising.

Courtesy of Kilmainham Gaol Museum, 17PC-IK43-12.

1 http://www.census.nationalarchives.ie/reels/nai000075502

Protecting Home Rule, defending the Empire, anti-German racism and avenging alleged German atrocities were all arguments used to stimulate recruitment to the British Army. The symbols of nationalist Ireland were mobilised in propaganda, as in the poster shown here. There was a surge of recruitment at the start of the war but it quickly dropped off and was poor outside the traditional urban centres. Between December 1914 and December 1915, in the entire province of Connacht, there were only 2,154 recruits enlisted into the British Army. Interestingly, this lack of support was not merely down to politics. Leitrim's 5,000 strong, largely Unionist, Protestant population supplied only thirty-six recruits in the same period.[1]

Courtesy of the National Library of Ireland, EPH 110.

1 B. Mac Giolla Choille, *Intelligence Notes, 1913–16* (Dublin, 1966), p. 182.

Social pressure and manipulation were also used to assist recruitment. Knowing the reluctance of farmers to enlist, some members of the western media and IPP politicians told audiences that there were plans among Britain's enemies to seize Irish land for their excess populations.[1] Republicans were called 'shirkers' and their manliness questioned. Galway city Republican Tom Courtney filled in enlistment forms using the names of prominent recruiters who were yet to sign up themselves, which led to them being called up.[2]

Courtesy of the National Library of Ireland, EPH 097.

Republicans disrupted recruiting meetings, and this led to physical confrontations with both the police and supporters of the army and the IPP. One meeting in the Town Hall in Galway was abandoned when Republicans exploded stink bombs, causing a stampede and making the hall unusable.[3] A number of Republicans served jail sentences for disrupting meetings, including Williamstown (G) man Jack Comer (*right*), a medical student.[4]

Courtesy of Dr Tim and Declan Horgan.

1 W. Henry, *Galway and the Great War* (Cork, 2006), pp. 44–50, 59.
2 Thomas Courtney, BMH WS 447, p. 21.
3 Thomas Hynes, BMH WS 714, pp. 2–3.
4 County Inspector's Reports Galway West Riding, October and November 1918 (The National Archives (TNA): Public Records Office (PRO) CO 904/107).

Pictured is William O'Malley, IPP MP for Connemara and a stalwart recruiter, in 1915. His son Willie decided to enlist. Writing about others joining up before him, he said: 'to hide behind their courage and their guns would be an overwhelming shame.' He was killed in action in France on 9 April 1917.[1] Note the message in the photograph on the horse's rug: 'WE ARE NOT SINN FEINERS'. This is to make sure that any onlookers do not mistake these National Volunteers for Irish Volunteers.

Courtesy of Getty Images.

1 W. Henry, *Forgotten Heroes: Galway Soldiers of the Great War 1914–1918* (Cork, 2007), p. 199.

Following the split in the Volunteer organisation, the Irish Volunteers reorganised and began recruiting and training new members. A group of them at a camp near Athlone is shown here. In the back row, fourth from the left, is J. J. 'Ginger' O'Connell, born in Mayo but later involved with the Republican movement in Sligo, who was in charge of the camp. To the right of O'Connell is Peter Paul Galligan of Carrigallen (LM) who was involved with the Volunteers in Dublin. Beside him is Larry Lardner of Athenry (G), who was the officer commanding the Volunteers in County Galway.

The leadership of the Irish Volunteers had been infiltrated by the IRB, with the aim of using that body in their planned uprising. To further the chance of success for this uprising, the IRB also appointed Sir Roger Casement to arrange a landing of German arms. One Galway police informer described Casement 'visiting all the important harbours from Carraroe to Leenane', presumably as part of his efforts to identify suitable locations for this.[1] Casement was later captured after landing in Kerry from a German submarine just before the Rising and was executed in August 1916. One of the policemen who was promoted as a result of Casement's arrest was John Kearney, who became a district inspector in Boyle (RN). During the War of Independence he provided the IRA with ammunition and intelligence as well as protecting the arrested.[2]

Courtesy of Kilmainham Gaol Museum, 16PO-1A23-19.

1 File on P. O'Malley MP: Firing on Police (TNA: PRO WO 35/102).

2 Letter from Pádraig Ó Dulchaointe, Brigade IO (P80/709, Desmond Fitzgerald Papers, UCD Archives).

The Irish Volunteers were supported by two auxiliary forces. One was Cumann na mBan, created to prepare nationalist women for key supporting roles in the event of the Volunteers being involved in warfare. The other, Na Fianna Éireann, was a nationalist scouting organisation, created and led by Countess de Markievicz, pictured here in Dublin with a group of Fianna members.

The Fianna organisation doesn't seem to have been particularly widespread in Connacht, but it did play a key role in the political development of many of the men from the Westport (MO) area who later made up one of the most important units of the West Mayo Brigade, IRA.[1]

Courtesy of Kilmainham Gaol Museum, 13PC-1A45-29.

1 Augusteijn, *From Public Defiance to Guerrilla Warfare*, p. 50.

Roger Casement, wearing a dark civilian coat and no cap, is pictured on the conning tower of the German submarine in which he travelled to Kerry during the attempted landing of arms for the Easter Rising.

Courtesy of Mercier Archives.

The failure to land arms, and a series of vague and countermanding orders, disrupted the Rising which broke out at Easter 1916. There was little activity outside Dublin, although there was more activity in County Galway than in most of the other counties in Ireland. In Dublin the rebels held out for a week, after which time their leadership agreed to surrender.

Incorrectly described as a 'Sinn Féin' Rising, the actions of the Volunteers were not supported by the majority of people at first. However, some did feel a sense of pride at the bravery shown by the rebels under fire, and the executions of sixteen of the rebel leaders, including Casement, quickly altered the initial hostility towards them to a feeling of anger against the British authorities and sympathy for the rebels. One of those executed was Major John MacBride from Westport (MO). MacBride had fought with the rebels based in Jacob's Biscuit Factory in Dublin during the Rising. He had also fought the British in the Boer War in South Africa, where he is pictured (*standing at the extreme right*) with a group of officers of the Irish Brigade.

Courtesy of Kilmainham Gaol Museum, 17PO-1A24-10.

Another of the executed rebels was Éamonn Ceannt from Ballymoe (G), a leading IRB member and Volunteer leader. He was in command of the Volunteer force that took over and held the South Dublin Union during the Rising.

Courtesy of Mercier Archives.

The most prominent female involved in the Rising was Countess Constance de Markievicz, a Protestant from Sligo. She was involved with the Irish Citizen Army and was second-in-command to Michael Mallin at St Stephen's Green during the Rising. Although she had initially been sentenced to death, her sentence was commuted to life in prison because of her gender. She was later elected to the Dublin constituency of St Patrick's and became Minister for Labour in the First Dáil.

Courtesy of Mercier Archives.

The only significant rebel activity in Connacht was in the area directly east of Galway city. There the Rising was led by IRB man Liam Mellows, an Irish Volunteer organiser who had been sent from Dublin in the aftermath of the 1914 split to reorganise and train the Volunteers in Galway.

Courtesy of Kilmainham Gaol Museum, 13PC-3N26-10.

One of the attacks carried out during the Rising in Galway was an assault on the police barracks at Clarenbridge (*left*). The barracks at Oranmore was also attacked, and a policeman was killed in a shoot-out at Carnmore.

Supporters of the IPP and Unionists were outraged at the rebellion and public bodies condemned the Rising. In Galway city a public meeting declared: 'we call on the authorities and people of Galway to co-operate to crush by every means the efforts of the disaffected fanatics and mischief-makers'.[1]

Author's collection.

1 A. Mitchell and P. Ó Snodaigh, *Irish Political Documents 1916–1949* (Dublin, 1985), p. 21.

Despite being far better armed and equipped, British forces failed to engage in any meaningful way with the Galway rebels. An attempt was made to shell the rebels from Galway Bay, probably from the *Laburnum* (*pictured*). The shelling had no impact on them but, unsure of events nationally, poorly armed and with little food or equipment, the rebels dispersed when they learned of the surrender in Dublin. When this happened, Mellows and several other senior figures went on the run in South Galway and Clare and eventually escaped to America.[1]

Courtesy of Mercier Archives.

All over Galway Republicans were arrested after the Rising ended. Many were kept in ships in Galway Bay, including the *Gloucester* (*pictured*) from which 100 marines had been landed for potential deployment against the rebel force.[2]

Courtesy of the Imperial War Museum.

1 'I Remember Mellows' by Proinsias Ó hEidhin. A copy of this document was kindly provided by historian Conor McNamara.

2 TNA: PRO WO 35/69/9.

Many who had taken no part in the Rising but were involved in radical politics or held radical views were also arrested. Amongst them were Joe Ring (*pictured*) and others from Westport (MO). One of those active in the arrest of Mayo Republicans was J. C. Milling, resident magistrate, whose dedication to duty led to his being shot dead in March 1919.[1]

Courtesy of Michael Ring, TD.

British forces guarding prisoners, probably in Richmond Barracks, Dublin, where a large number of rural Volunteers were held before transfer to British prisons. The crown forces had mixed feelings about the Rising. Pádraig Ó Fathaigh from Ballycahalan, Gort (G), commented: 'The RIC were most bitter and vindictive, on the other hand the military, both Irish and English & Scotch, were friendly and sympathetic'.[2] In Nottingham, prisoner Mick Newell from Castlegar (G) witnessed a member of the British Army striking three members of a hostile crowd who gathered around the rebel prisoners, and shouting: 'Up Carraroe, Up Connemara'.[3]

Courtesy of Kilmainham Gaol Museum, 17PC-1A44-21.

1 Price, *The Flame and the Candle*, pp. 29–33.

2 T. McMahon, *Pádraig Ó Fathaigh's War of Independence: Recollections of a Galway Gaelic Leaguer* (Cork, 2000), p. 38.

3 Mick Newell, BMH WS 342, p. 8.

Frongoch Internment Camp, Wales. After being dispersed to a number of British prisons, the vast majority of Republican prisoners were gathered together in this old distillery, which had, until recently, housed German prisoners of war. After Dublin, Galway had the largest number of men arrested in the aftermath of the Easter Rising, with 322 of them being interned in Frongoch; Mayo had thirty-seven, Sligo eleven, Roscommon eight and Leitrim five. The prisoners busied themselves in the camp expressing their sporting, academic and artistic talents, their political opinions and their wit. In the camp new leaders for the Republican movement emerged, mistakes were analysed, military strategy was taught and contacts were established. At home sympathy and respect for the rebels was daily increasing. By Christmas 1916 all the Frongoch prisoners had been released and allowed to return to Ireland.

Courtesy of Kilmainham Gaol Museum, 18PC-1D54-04.

This photograph of released prisoners taken in Dublin in 1917 contains a number of the men who had taken part in the Rising in Galway, as well as a number of westerners who had taken part in the Rising elsewhere.

Three cases of particular interest are standing in the back row. Fourth from the left is Michael (Miko) Fleming from Clarenbridge (G). From a staunchly Republican family, Fleming was one of six brothers who were 'out' in the Rising. Their father, who had amassed a private collection of weapons in the hope that there would eventually be a rebellion, also took part and was interned.

Fifth from the right is Willie Hussey. After the Rising an RIC man who had been a prisoner of the rebels attempted to help Hussey by testifying that Hussey had also been a prisoner. Hussey's contradiction of the RIC man's testimony earned him a five-year sentence.[1]

Fifth from the left is Peter Paul Galligan of Carrigallen (LM), who attempted to prevent British troops travelling from Wexford to Dublin to oppose the Rising.

Courtesy of Kilmainham Gaol Museum, 18PO-IA51-17.

1 *Connacht Tribune* accounts of the Rising, 9 and 16 April 1966; C. D. Greaves, *Liam Mellows and the Irish Revolution* (Belfast, 2004), p. 88.

The senior Republican prisoners were released in June 1917 after a general amnesty and received with euphoria on their arrival back in Ireland. Here Countess de Markievicz is seen on her return to Dublin. In Sligo she received the freedom of the borough for 'her action in the cause of liberty'.[1]

Courtesy of Kilmainham Gaol Museum, 18PC-1A25-14.

To consolidate their new strength Republicans began to run candidates in parliamentary by-elections in 1917–18. Part of their strategy was to actively seek candidates who were linked with the Easter Rising. In North Roscommon the candidate selected to contest the 1917 by-election on behalf of the Republicans was veteran nationalist George Noble, Count Plunkett, seen here with his son, Joseph Mary, who was executed after the Rising. Count Plunkett won the seat comfortably.

Courtesy of Kilmainham Gaol Museum, 13PC-1K43-11.

1 Farry, *Sligo 1914–1921*.

Other than the Rising, however, there were various reasons for the growth in support for the more radical nationalists, including the association of the IPP with British recruitment, anger about partition, lack of progress on land redistribution and instances of corruption. Brian Cusack (*above right*) was elected in the 1918 general election as a Sinn Féin candidate for North Galway, defeating the IPP candidate. Prior to this, while seeking a job working for a local government body dominated by the IPP, Cusack, a medical doctor, was repeatedly told: 'That will cost you a bit of money.' Cusack got the job without resorting to bribery.[1]

Courtesy of Kilmainham Gaol Museum, 2010.0005.

1 Brian Cusack, BMH WS 736, p. 9.

One of the noticeable characteristics of the revolutionary period in the west was the support which young clergymen such as Father Michael O'Flanagan (curate in Crossna (RN)) gave to the Republican movement.[1] An Irish language enthusiast and a land radical, he told Crossna Sinn Féin club in 1917 that grazing farms should be bought and 'divided into reasonably sized tillage farms'.[2]

Courtesy of Kilmainham Gaol Museum.

There were food shortages as a result of the First World War and the Republican movement also gained support by actively seeking to remedy the situation. In Mayo food was collected from farmers who provided it voluntarily and distributed among the urban poor.[3] George Plunkett (*left, image taken in the 1940s*), another son of Count Plunkett, took part in one land seizure directed at 100 acres owned by Lord Kingston in Arigna (RN). Three hundred men assembled with tools. A large number of policemen barred the way. At a signal from Plunkett the local men started to dig to prepare the land for planting crops, against the wishes of the owner. They were baton charged and Plunkett received a jail term.[4]

Courtesy of Honor Ó Brolchain.

1 M. Moran, *Executed for Ireland: The Patrick Moran Story* (Cork, 2010), p. 56.

2 Campbell, *Land and Revolution*, p. 241.

3 Augusteijn, *From Public Defiance to Guerrilla Warfare*, p. 256.

4 K. Hegarty Thorne, *They Put the Flag a-Flyin': The Roscommon Volunteers 1916–1923* (Oregon, 2007), pp. 14–15.

A native of Mayo, Kathleen Lynn was the daughter of a Church of Ireland clergyman. A medical doctor, a socialist and a feminist, she played an active role in the Irish Citizen Army in Dublin and was involved in the Rising. Following the Rising radical Republicans joined Sinn Féin rather than start their own party and there was a certain amount of tension between the radical and moderate wings, and also between economic radicals and conservatives. In 1917 Easter Rising veteran Éamon de Valera became president, founder Arthur Griffith became vice-president and Kathleen Lynn was elected to the party's executive committee.

Courtesy of Kilmainham Gaol Museum, 17PO-IB52-13.

Ned Walsh, a Volunteer from Spiddal (G). The RIC viewed with unease the Republican movement's growing confidence. One intelligence report described events in Spiddal in 1917, when local Republicans assembled for drilling:

> Ned Walsh called for three cheers for De Valera. For an Irish Republic. For Easter Week. For Kilkenny [where Sinn Féin had won a by-election]. He also held a Sinn Féin flag for some time. Patrick Costello and Joseph Thornton were throwing oil on the fire. James Flaherty carried a Sinn Féin flag also, after some time the party came on to the road in answer to a whistle and I heard James Flaherty call out to the crowd 'Fall in in fours' which they did and marched through the village past the Barracks and Post Office.[1]

Courtesy of the Breathnach family.

1 County Galway: Drilling, Wearing Uniform etc., RIC report, 12 August 1917 (TNA: PRO WO 35/97).

Following the release of the Easter Rising prisoners, the Volunteers began to reorganise. Old companies were re-established and new ones created, while active recruiting began for new membership. Amongst the new members in Galway were Pat (*left in this commemorative card*) and Harry (*right*) Loughnane of Shanaglish near Gort (G). 'It grieves me to think that we stood by while others suffered. If I only got the least inkling of the Rising and what Sinn Féin stood for, I, too, would have done my part' was Pat's comment on the Rising. Pat became an officer in the local IRA company and president of the local Sinn Féin cumann, with Harry as its secretary.[1]

Courtesy of NUI Galway.

It wasn't easy to make soldiers of the new Volunteers, and organisers were sent from Irish Volunteer headquarters in Dublin to help reorganise and train the rural companies. Mayo-born Ernie O'Malley, sent to Roscommon as a Republican organiser, became the most famous of these.

Courtesy of Cormac O'Malley.

1 C. O'Malley and C. Ó Comhraí, *The Men Will Talk to Me: Galway Interviews by Ernie O'Malley* (Cork, 2013), p. 31.

he Police, having no useful employment, spend their time in country places sneaking round spying upon the people.

One of the major issues that organisers had to contend with was fear of the RIC. They were nicknamed 'The eyes and ears of Dublin Castle', and their ability to gather intelligence was legendary, as this cartoon shows; this annoyed and intimidated nationalists and Republicans. Ernie O'Malley wrote of the Volunteers he had been sent to reorganise: 'Companies in South Roscommon suffer severely from spy mania. The individual Volunteers distrust their officers and each other.'[1] While suspicions could easily be dismissed as paranoia, the Volunteers were right to be careful. During the War of Independence an IRA South Roscommon Brigade Intelligence Officer was unmasked as a British agent.[2]

Courtesy of Mercier Archives.

Growing violence against the police was not restricted to men. A police report from 25 August 1918 describes how a group of Cumann na mBan members from Galway city marched out to Barna under the command of an IRA Volunteer, Henry Shiels, as well as Eileen Keane of Eyre Square and Mary Malone of Dominick Street. When the police arrested Shiels the barracks windows were smashed.[3] Pictured is the Barna Barracks building as it is in 2013.

Courtesy of Joe O'Connor.

1 Report on the Intelligence Branch Chief of Police, Dublin Castle, May 1920-July 1921, p. 23 (TNA: PRO WO 35/214).

2 Thomas Crawley, BMH WS 718, p. 15.

3 County Galway Drilling, Wearing Uniform etc. (TNA: PRO WO 35/97).

Arrested Republicans were defiant and belligerent. When eight men from the Ballymote (SO) area were tried for land agitation in February 1918, they refused to stand or remove their caps for the judge, passed cigarettes around and sang Republican ballads.[1] This defiance was essential to Republican morale.

When fellow Sligo Republican Billy Pilkington (*pictured*) was arrested and convicted for unlawful assembly in Sligo in April 1919:

> … the defendant's mother entered the court, and addressing the figure in the dock, asked, 'Did you give bail?'
>
> The defendant replied, 'No.'
>
> 'Good,' said the mother. 'If you did I would not let you into the house again.'[2]

Pilkington went on to take an active part in the War of Independence and Civil War, during which he was officer commanding the IRA's 3rd Western Division of Sligo, North Leitrim and a portion of Fermanagh.

Courtesy of Mercier Archives.

1 *The Freeman's Journal*, 28 February 1918.

2 P. Hart, *The I.R.A. and its Enemies* (Oxford, 1998), p. 175.

Despite the massive surge in Republican support, many in the west remained hostile to the Volunteers. Republicans were dismissive of the character and patriotism of 'big farmers' and garrison towns such as Athlone and Boyle (RN) because of the lack of support received from townspeople and the better off.[1] In Galway city the RIC noted that only the university was a 'hotbed of Sinn Féinism'.[2] Engineering students and medical students such as Conchubhar Ó Laoghaire from Spiddal (G) dominated the university company of the Irish Volunteers.

Courtesy of Mártan Ó Ciardha.

A number of the university staff, such as Tomás Ó Máille, also openly identified with the Republican movement. Ó Máille was Professor of Irish at the university during the revolutionary years.

Courtesy of An Gúm.

1 Henry O'Brien, BMH WS 1308, p. 4; James Feely, BMH WS 997, p. 11.

2 County Inspector's Report Galway West Riding, February 1917 (TNA: PRO CO 904/102).

As much as from political convictions, some members joined the Republican movement for its camaraderie and the excitement that went with it. Above is a Sinn Féin cycle club from East Mayo. Like cultural organisations, political organisations were a vital component of the social lives of many people on limited incomes and provided the opportunity to combine charity work, hobbies and cultural activities with political activism.

Courtesy of Kilmainham Gaol Museum, 13PD-1A11-14.

Following the death of John Redmond early in 1918, John Dillon became leader of the IPP. This picture was taken in Enniskillen at his first public meeting as leader. By this time the IPP was beginning to regain lost ground against Sinn Féin. Arms raids, land seizures and the threat of another rising terrified the better off and more moderate Sinn Féin supporters. To many these actions brought to mind Russia, where the communist Bolsheviks had seized power in 1917.

Courtesy of Kilmainham Gaol Museum, 18PO-1A31-02.

The IPP's resurgence was short-lived. Faced with a major German offensive in the spring of 1918 the British government began to prepare for conscription in Ireland. This was greeted with outrage by nationalists and Republicans, and Sinn Féin's popularity was quickly reignited. All nationalist parties and organisations, including the IPP, opposed conscription. In the picture above Sinn Féin leader Éamon de Valera and IPP leader John Dillon are seated side by side at an anti-conscription rally in Ballaghderreen (RN).

However, it was the Irish Volunteers who were perceived to be in a position to offer something more effective than words as a protest against the policy, and its ranks were flooded with new members.

When the government was forced to shelve the plan as a response to the determined opposition it faced in Ireland, this became a major propaganda victory for the Volunteers and Sinn Féin.

Courtesy of Mercier Archives.

The British government, determined to avoid another uprising, appointed Sir John French as Lord Lieutenant, the King's representative in Ireland. This signalled a hardening of the government's attitude towards radical nationalism. French was a military man whose ability had been questioned during the First World War, so Ireland offered him an opportunity to redeem himself. His first significant act was to arrest Republican leaders for their alleged involvement in the 'German Plot', as the British government suspected an impending uprising with German assistance. Nationalist Ireland was sceptical. Before the arrests were carried out, details were leaked and a number of key radicals avoided arrest. This allowed them to increase their control of Sinn Féin and the Irish Volunteers.[1]

Courtesy of Mercier Archives.

1 M. Foy, *Michael Collins's Intelligence War* (Gloucestershire, 2006), pp. 13–15.

Not all prominent Republicans managed to avoid arrest and their incarceration further hardened nationalist opinion. Plans, that ultimately came to nothing, were well advanced to import German weapons into Inverin (G).[1] Amongst the locals involved in the planning was Volunteer Peadar Ó Máille (*left*). The British were apparently informed of the plan and the arms dumped at sea.

Courtesy of Peadar Óg Ó Máille.

In November 1918 the First World War came to an end, with Britain and her Allies triumphant. Often unskilled, Great War veterans returning to Ireland struggled to find regular employment. Alcoholism, petty crime, venereal disease, domestic disharmony and even serious domestic violence became a feature of some of their lives. Many were forced into poverty in a society that had changed massively since they left for war. Some clashed with the Volunteers in urban areas for political reasons or as the Volunteers enforced the law, while others were suspected of informing on the Volunteers and a small number were executed as informers. However, being an ex-soldier also offered little protection against British excesses. In Roscommon an ex-soldier was allegedly compelled to accompany British forces during raids to protect the identity of their local guide, and this led to his wrongful execution by the IRA as a suspected informer.[2] A minority became involved in the conflict. Michael Higgins (*top*) from Boyle (RN) and Michael Fitzgerald (*bottom*) of Ahascragh (G) both joined the RIC. Fitzgerald later resigned and joined an IRA unit in Roscommon.[3]

Image of Higgins courtesy of Martin Higgins; image of Fitzgerald courtesy of J. Anthony Gaughan.

1 Mícheál Ó Droighneáin, BMH WS 1718, pp. 5–6.

2 Matthew Davis, BMH WS 691, p. 7.

3 For an examination of Fitzgerald's career see J. A. Gaughan, *The Memoirs of Constable Jeremiah Mee* (Cork, 2012).

In 1918 a general election was called, which saw the mobilisation of thousands of Republicans who canvassed for Republican candidates, protected Republican speakers, transported voters to the polls and in some cases voted more than once. Pictured is the South Galway Sinn Féin election committee, 1918.

Standing, left to right: Rev. J. W. O'Meehan, James Hogan, Rev. M. C. O'Farrell, Peter Sweeney, Paddy Hogan and James Flynn.

Seated: Martin Forde, Martin Ryan, Rev. J. Dunne and Laurence Carty.

This picture encapsulates the disparate coalition of forces that made up the Republican movement in the west – the priests; Sweeney, the long-time Republican; the Hogans, part of the prosperous Catholic middle class that had been waiting to take over the reins in a Dublin parliament; James Flynn, a returned Frongoch internee; and Martin Forde, leader of the Kilchreest land committee which had purchased land for redistribution.[1]

Courtesy of Kilmainham Gaol Museum, 18PO-1A31-07.

1 Campbell, *Land and Revolution*, p. 244.

An Bodaċ Bréan

"Cé hé an Bodaċ breilleaċ bréan
D'innis bréag fá luċt tír-ġráḋa
Nuair a h-iarraḋ Cuing na nGall
Réabaḋ ṫall ar páipéar an áir?

An Feallṫóir sé Máirtín Mór
Árd a ġlór i n-aġaiḋ Gaeḋeal
Má ṁaireann aon fear díob beo
Is leis is ró-ṁór an sgéul!

Nuair tógaiġeaḋ ar an ngleo
Rinne Mór leis an ARM Dubh
An Dream a Cuireaḋ i mbruid
Máirtín a ṫug leis gá luaḋ!

'Sé a ġríosaiġ an Píleár HEARS
Cleaċt ceird an feallṫóir cruaiḋe
Cuir sé iomḋa coir n-a ṫeiġ
Mian leis a mbeiṫ fan uaiġ.

Cá raċaiḋ an Bodaċ Bréan?
Cun an Ifrinn féin is teo.
Béiḋ diabail gá cur i gcóir
Ar a ṫóin beiḋ lasair beo!

Seaġán na Sagart Éirinn ann!
Clann CAREY dá mbruiġ fá réir.
Sgríobhann PIGGOTT dá ndóġ meall,
Diarmaid na nGall leo go léir!

Bacfar Máirtín go beiṫ in am
Cruaḋlaoċ, TOM, gur Coisḋlá Saoġlaċ
Beiḋ Diabail ag béartáll YOUNG
Ag clann Donnḋa Fágtar Laoileaċ.

With little access to a media controlled by their political opponents, and in an age where there were still high levels of illiteracy, Republicans utilised visual propaganda and songs to increase their support. Pictured is an Irish-language Republican ballad or poem criticising IPP stalwart Máirtín Mór McDonogh, a major Galway businessman with links to Connemara. Crown forces seized this copy of the ballad during a raid in Galway.

Courtesy of the National Archives, Kew, George Nicolls, PRO WO 35/142.

Above is another example of Republican propaganda from this period. In Ireland the election became a referendum on the national question and on the performance of the IPP in the previous years. Sinn Féin portrayed themselves as honourable and idealistic and the IPP as jaded and corrupted. They also highlighted the changing of world politics as a result of peace settlements following the end of the First World War, and the apparent disaster that British rule had been for the Irish both demographically and economically.[1]

Courtesy of Kilmainham Gaol Museum, 18PD-1A14-27.

1 *Connacht Tribune*, 7, 14 December 1918.

IPP speakers emphasised what they saw as the impracticality of Sinn Féin's plans to withdraw from the British parliament and establish a republic. The IPP also sought to represent Sinn Féin's expansion as the rebellion of the young against their more sensible elders. One South Mayo IPP figure told an audience at Shrule that there were men: 'who told their fathers that they knew more about their business than they themselves do, and they told their fathers that if they attempted to vote for him they would lock them up in barns.'[1] In this cartoon a Sinn Féin propagandist has turned the accusation of impracticality back onto the IPP.

Courtesy of Kilmainham Gaol Museum, 18PD-1A14-26.

1 *Connacht Tribune*, 7, 14 December 1918.

While a vote for Sinn Féin was not a vote for a declaration of war against Britain, a future rising by Republicans was a very real possibility. Many of the candidates selected had been involved in the Easter Rising with several of them being on the run at the time of the election. Pictured on the left is Harry Boland, a Dublin Easter Rising veteran with Roscommon roots, who was selected as the Sinn Féin candidate for Roscommon South. Also pictured is a mugshot of another veteran of the Dublin Rising, Galway South candidate, Frank Fahy, originally from Kilchreest (G). On 14 December Ireland went to the polls and the resounding victory for Sinn Féin was a herald of things to come.

Courtesy of Kilmainham Gaol Museum, 2012.0106 and 17PO-1A24-14.

THE REPUBLIC REALISED: 1919–21

On applying to the RIC for protection they informed me that they were unable to protect themselves and could do nothing for me.

Galway cattle grazier Frederick Homan Falkiner writing about the War of Independence.[1]

Having taken 73 out of 105 available seats in the 1918 election, the Sinn Féin MPs created their own parliament known as Dáil Éireann. Pictured are the TDs who were at the first meeting in January 1919, including Count Plunkett (Roscommon North) and Pádraic Ó Máille (Connemara) (*seated fourth and seventh from the left respectively*). Also in the picture is Dr John Crowley (Mayo North) (*fifth from right, standing*). The Dáil affirmed the creation of the Republic that had been declared during Easter Week, outlined their vision of the future and sought international recognition. This was received in the press with both cynicism and fear.[2] They were

1 Frederick Homan Falkiner (TNA: PRO CO 762/183).

2 A. Mitchell, *Revolutionary Government in Ireland: Dáil Éireann 1919–22* (Dublin, 1995), p. 19.

serious, however, and to raise funds organised a highly successful loan by appealing to the public, with the parliamentary constituency of Mayo South topping the collection for Connacht in mid-1920.[3] Efforts were made to aid economic initiatives, promote Gaelic culture, develop an alternative legal system and solve the Land Question. The Irish Volunteers were renamed the Irish Republican Army (IRA) and Dáil control was, theoretically, imposed on them.

On the same day that the Dáil first met, the first shots were fired in the War of Independence, at Soloheadbeg, Tipperary.

Courtesy of Mercier Archives.

There was real anger and fear about British plans to introduce partition in order to satisfy Ulster Unionist demands, with the *Church of Ireland Gazette* declaring that 'Permanent partition is a thing of evil'.[4] In December 1919 a popular boycott of goods from Belfast Unionist firms was initiated in Tuam (G) as a protest against partition. It soon became a protest against anti-Catholic violence in the north-east. Eventually the Sinn Féin leadership, keen to avoid anything that looked like religious conflict, reluctantly endorsed it.[5] One of those who became involved in enforcing the boycott was an ex-member of the RIC, Jeremiah Mee from Glenamaddy (G). Mee was a hate figure for supporters of the crown forces because of his role in a protest by policemen against the divisional commissioner in Listowel, Kerry, where the policemen claimed they had been encouraged to shoot people acting suspiciously without fear of consequences. The public were sceptical about official denials and the commissioner was later shot dead by the IRA in Cork city.[6]

Courtesy of J. Anthony Gaughan.

3 *Ibid.*, p. 64.

4 *Church of Ireland Gazette*, 12 March 1920.

5 Mitchell, *Revolutionary Government*, pp. 168–72.

6 M. Hopkinson, *The Irish War of Independence* (Dublin 2002), p. 89.

The Labour Party and Sinn Féin had co-operated during the 1918 election and some IRA men were Labour Party rather than Sinn Féin members. Sligo Labour leader and trade unionist John Lynch (*left*) served three months imprisonment for a Republican speech given in Boyle (RN) in September 1918.[1] Throughout the period of the War of Independence politically motivated strikes hampered the ability of the British to function, most famously when the country's railway workers refused to transport armed members of the security forces. In revenge British forces targeted trade unionists during reprisals.

Courtesy of Betty McGowan.

Early IRA attacks on the crown forces were largely limited to neutralising British intelligence and seizing arms. On 19 December 1919 the IRA came close to a significant coup with the attempted assassination of Sir John French. The IRA monitored his movements constantly, with particular attention being paid to his property at Drumdoe (RN). Word reached the IRA that French would leave Roscommon for the Vice-Regal Lodge in the Phoenix Park. The assassination attempt failed and Martin Savage (*left*), an Easter Rising veteran from Ballisodare (SO), was killed.

Courtesy of Mercier Archives.

1 For more on Lynch see Farry, *Sligo 1914–1921*.

As violence intensified, raids by security forces also increased, becoming a regular feature of life in Republican areas. Raids and searches were an inconvenience in the early part of the war and did not yet inspire the terror that would later become associated with them. Rather than turning people against the Republicans, the raids alienated people from the British. Pictured are a British Army checkpoint at Athlone (*above*) and the British Army searching through turf for arms somewhere in North Connacht.

Courtesy of Athlone Library [checkpoint] and Bedfordshire and Luton Archives Service X550-2-6_p47a.

There were a lot of guns in the Irish countryside, although they were not necessarily of great quality. For the most part weapons were simply handed over and Republicans often made an effort to minimise the threatening nature of the raids they carried out for guns. One member of the landed class in East Galway wrote about the IRA 'very considerately leaving two (boxes of ammunition) for shooting purposes'.[1] Violence could also be a feature of the raids, however. One Leitrim Volunteer later wrote: 'Generally, and particularly amongst the Catholic population, it was only a matter of asking them for their guns, but some of the Protestant and Unionist elements had to be persuaded to do so [hand them over] by rougher methods.'[2]

While this is perhaps an accurate description of the situation in Leitrim, there doesn't seem to have been a connection elsewhere between religion and a tendency to resist. The treatment of the Perceval family, a landed Protestant family at Templehouse in Sligo, at the hands of Republicans was generally reasonably positive. However, one occasion was brutally different and led to Nora (*pictured*) suffering a miscarriage. In her own words:

> ... my hands were twisted and tied behind my back and my arms above the elbows were tied with the rope; my rists [*sic*] were also tied at the same time with a piece of string; the cloth was tied over my eyes, and I was gaged [*sic*] by a filthy handkerchief being put into my mouth and tied behind my head; during the time that I was being tied I was kicked on the shins and the small of the back; they did not seem to care how they treated me.'[3]

It was thought that the fact that the raiders were strangers being guided by a dismissed employee contributed to the violence used during this episode.

Photograph and additional information courtesy of her grandson Sandy Perceval.

1 F. S. Chevers, *Chevers of Killyan*, p. 18 (NUI Galway LE (20) (1)).

2 Patrick Doherty, BMH WS 1195, pp. 5–6.

3 *Leitrim Observer*, 10 April 1920.

From January 1920 police barracks began to be attacked. From the Republican perspective this had the advantage of giving large numbers of men experience under fire and ensuring that the RIC felt safe nowhere. The disadvantage was that it wasted a lot of scarce ammunition with little hope of capturing weapons or ammunition. This picture shows Frenchpark RIC Barracks (RN) after it was attacked on 2 October 1920.

Courtesy of Bedfordshire and Luton Archives Service X550-2-6_p31.

Given the poor morale in the force, the bravery with which the RIC defended their barracks is noticeable. Sergeant Edward Brady received the pictured medal for his defence of Bookeen (G) RIC Barracks in July 1920. Even with the barracks on fire he refused to surrender and the policemen fought their way out of the barracks and escaped.[1]

Courtesy of Garda Museum.

1 *Connacht Tribune*, 10 July 1920.

There was tension in the Republican movement about the use of violence. The OC of the Galway Brigade, Seamus Murphy, frustrated the attempts of his more militant subordinates to initiate a guerrilla campaign. He broke the militant University College Galway Company of the Volunteers (*above*) after an attack on Lough George (G) RIC Barracks in May 1920 by court-martialling their officers.[1] Unsurprisingly tensions within the movement worsened as risk increased. In one case a Roscommon Volunteer prevented the IRA from ambushing the crown forces by passing false information. It was suspected that this was done to protect his house from reprisals that were likely to follow any ambush. The local IRA faced a dilemma:

> He was one of the original officers … and was well liked, and shooting him appeared drastic and might have local complications. Eventually it was decided that he would be dismissed from the Volunteers.[2]

Courtesy of NUI Galway.

1 O'Malley and Ó Comhraí, *The Men Will Talk to Me*, pp. 222–3.

2 Martin Fallon, BMH WS 1121, pp. 9–10.

As a result of the unsuitability of rural RIC barracks for defence against the IRA, many were abandoned and their garrisons were moved into urban areas. 424 abandoned barracks were torched by the IRA in a nationwide campaign beginning at Easter 1920, a telling reminder of the scale of their organisation.[1] To put the RIC's retreat into context, in 1920 Mayo had forty-seven police barracks. In 1921 it had twenty-three.[2] Pictured are the burned-out barracks at Keash (SO) (*top*) and at Cootehall (RN).

Courtesy of Bedfordshire and Luton Archives Service X550-2-6_p52a and X550-2-6_96a.

1 C. Townshend, *The British Campaign in Ireland, 1919–1921* (Oxford, 1975), p. 65.

2 D. Leeson, *The Black and Tans: British Police and Auxiliaries in the Irish War of Independence* (Oxford, 2011), p. 23.

Leading Republicans began to be arrested in early 1920 and effectively interned without trial. This led to hunger strikes in prisons in Ireland and Britain, including Galway Jail where a small number of Republican prisoners were being held. Amongst those who went on hunger strike in the jail was Colm Ó Gaora, an IRA man from Rosmuck (G) (*right*). When news of the strike broke a crowd gathered outside the prison and were led in prayer by Republican priests, among them Father Michael Griffin (*left*), a young curate from the Rahoon parish on the outskirts of Galway city. Griffin was a noted Irish-language enthusiast and Republican. As part of a national strike the city was shut down.[1] The authorities gave in to the pressure and the prisoners were released.

Ó Gaora courtesy of An Gúm; Griffin courtesy of Clare County Library.

1 *Connacht Tribune*, 17 April 1920.

Like the RIC, the judiciary, also seen as representatives of British interests, felt increasingly isolated. In Headford (G) 'Major Bourke RM attended at Headford Petty Sessions on Friday, but the only appearance was a young goat that stalked in as far as the witness table and quickly left.'[1] In Oughterard (G) one member of the judiciary, James Hill (*pictured*), had the following conversation with a defendant:

> (Hill) 'If you were in my boots what would you do?'
> 'God forbid I would be in your boots.'
> 'Wouldn't you think you would be safe?'
> 'I would not think so.'[2]

Courtesy of Police Museum, Belfast.

1 *Connacht Tribune*, 17 July 1920.

2 *Ibid.*, 20 March 1920.

Despite the events of the War of Independence, agrarian violence and land redistribution continued, with 4–5,000 acres reportedly being redistributed in South Sligo in 1919.[1] After two land murders in Galway an even greater explosion of land agitation occurred in 1920. *The Galway Express*, a Republican newspaper, claimed that 30,000 acres had been cleared of animals in Galway with the centre of the agitation being: 'Kilconnell-Ahascragh-Woodlawn'.[2] The owner of Castlegar House, Ahascragh (G) (*above*), was offered £4,000 to give up land at the height of the agitation, but he refused and saw his house attacked in 1922.[3]

At a local level Republicans were heavily involved in the agitation, but non-Republicans were also involved and anyone could be targeted, including members of the clergy. This threatened to split the Republican movement and derail the struggle for independence. The Republican chairman of Galway Urban District Council was beaten up because the council showed an interest in acquiring some land at Menlo for a public park. He was opposed by the Castlegar Republicans, whose leader, Brian Molloy, wrote to the council offering to meet them on behalf of the Menlo tenants. The chairman wasn't impressed: 'that letter read very courteously but the gentleman who wrote it used quite different language on Wednesday – in fact he did not care to say what his language had been.'[4]

Courtesy of the Irish Architectural Archive, 022_023_X_001.

1 Campbell, *Land and Revolution*, p. 243.

2 *The Galway Express*, 10 April 1920.

3 *Connacht Tribune*, 10 June 1922.

4 *The Galway Express*, 10 April 1920.

There was a long-running dispute about the lands around Clifden Castle. The secretary of the local Sinn Féin cumann wrote to his superior in Galway city:

> I am very much surprised that you didn't answer any of my letters with reference to the Castle lands. The tenants got so mad about your carelessness in the matter that they have cleared the lands themselves and the members of the Sinn Féin club don't know whether to assist them or not.[1]

The Dáil established Land Courts and a Land Bank during 1919–20 to facilitate the purchasing and peaceful transference of land. One Republican defined their role as: 'trying to ensure that the farmers' sons, the workers and others would have an opportunity of getting on the land'. Claimants were warned that threats were 'gravely to the prejudice of the claimants'.[2] Good prices for land and the fear that money might not be offered in the future made many landowners amenable to sale and some thousands of acres were transferred.

Courtesy of the Irish Architectural Archive, 022_031_X_001.

1 File on George Nicolls (TNA: PRO WO 35/142).

2 *The Galway Express*, 22 May 1920.

As early as 1917 Republicans, on their own initiative, had established a court in Ballaghdereen (RN) to provide an alternative to the British-controlled court system, with Oranmore and Kinvara (G) following suit early in 1918.[1] By 1920 the Dáil had established a formalised Republican court system in much of the country. Despite the fact that many of the people running these courts were not trained in the law, these institutions provided effective propaganda for the Republican cause, as efforts were made to ensure that all the people who used them were fairly treated, regardless of background or politics. Punishments handed down by the courts included removal to an isolated area for brief imprisonment, fines, compulsory labour and exile. The picture shows the Dáil court at Westport (MO). The three judges who tried this case were John O'Boyle (Mayo County Council), Conor A. Maguire (chairman of Mayo County Council) and Ned Moane (IRA officer). J. C. Garvey and John Gibbons were solicitors and one of the two Republican policemen standing guard in the centre aisle when this photograph was taken was Seán Gibbons.[2]

Courtesy of Kilmainham Gaol Museum, 19PC-1A46-05.

1 Sinn Féin Arbitration Court (TNA: PRO CO 904/24 (2)).

2 Price, *The Flame and the Candle: War in Mayo 1919–1924*, p. 76.

The Republican judiciary were respected members of the community, such as Tom Dillon (*left*), a university professor in Galway city, and Dan Corry (*right*), a Loughrea (G) shopkeeper. Priests and women also featured among the judges. Good judgement was essential. In one famous case at Two Mile Ditch, Castlegar (G), two brothers fell out over the division of land. It was felt that the older brother was bullying the younger brother. The decision of the court was that the older brother should divide the land as he saw fit. Delighted, he drew the border to ensure that one farm got the good land and the other farm got the poor land. The court then allowed the younger brother to choose the portion he wanted.[1]

Tom Dillon courtesy of Honor Ó Brolchain; Dan Corry courtesy of the Corry family.

1 Patrick Moylett, BMH WS 767, pp. 25–6.

Members of the Volunteers were appointed as part of a new Irish Republican Police force. Note the IRP initials around the cuff of Westport (MO) Volunteer John Gannon's jacket. These Republican Police had the advantage of local knowledge and they enthusiastically implemented the law. Their enforcement of the licensing laws and their suppression of the illegal poteen trade caused some friction, but also gained them praise. In some cases the RIC attempted to persuade criminals to inform on Republican policemen, but they had few successes. For example, when the RIC arrested Republicans who had themselves arrested suspected thieves in Carraroe (G), the thieves 'stated to the police that they were taken out of their beds but would not state why and said they did not know the men who took them out of bed'.[1]

Courtesy of John Gannon's grandnephew John Francis Gannon. © John Francis Gannon.

1 *The Galway Express*, 28 August 1920 and 4 September 1920; George Staunton, BMH WS 453, p. 9; Courts Martial John Keane, Bartley Flaherty, Michael Keane and Patrick O'Malley (TNA: PRO WO 35/114).

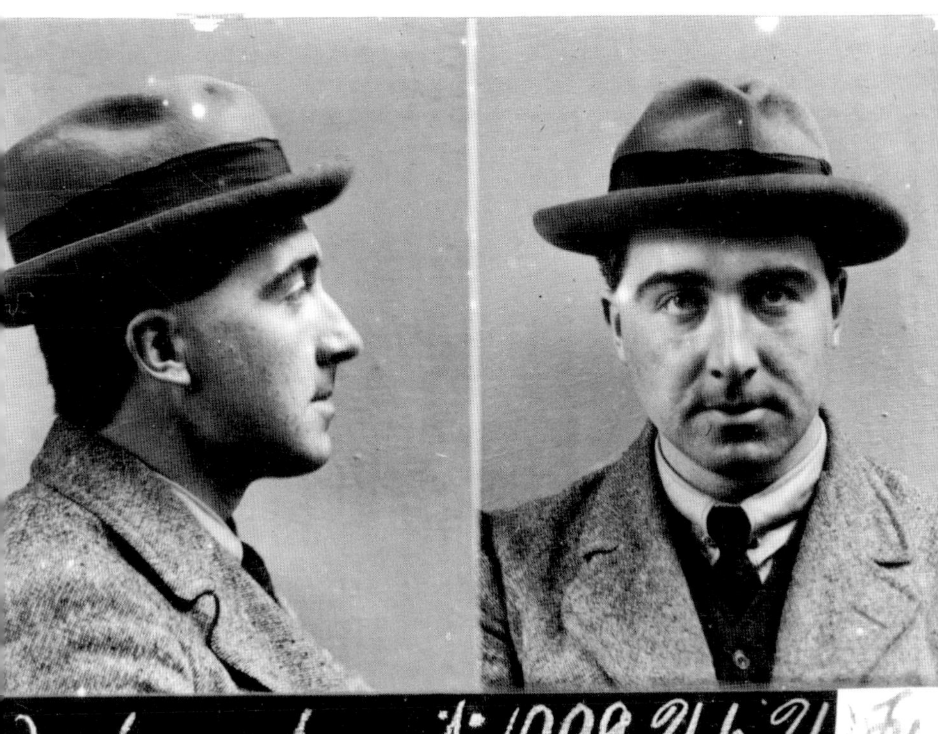

Sligo man Frank Carty, commandant of the Tubbercurry Battalion, IRA, played a game of cat and mouse with British forces in 1920–21. Sprung from Sligo Jail by the local IRA, he was later re-arrested and imprisoned in Derry where he escaped from the jail's hospital wing. Making his way to Glasgow he was again arrested. An attempt to rescue him from a prison van resulted in the death of a police inspector and sectarian rioting, but the British held on to their man. He was sent to Mountjoy Jail in Dublin, where this photograph was taken and he was held to the end of the War of Independence.[1]

Courtesy of National Archives of Ireland: D/Justice, Mountjoy Jail-2001/124/2/68.

1 Farry, *Sligo 1914–1921*.

IRA units in Britain were a key component of Republican efforts to acquire arms. While IRA men in Britain were often emigrants that wasn't necessarily the case. This photograph is of members of the IRA after their release from Dartmoor Prison. Amongst them, seated on the far right, is John Pinkman, who was arrested for his part in an arson campaign around Liverpool, where he was born. His parents hailed from Glenade and Kilclare in Leitrim.

The relationship between the IRA in the west of Ireland and a Munster-dominated IRA GHQ in Dublin was poor. Feeling discriminated against in the allocation of resources, western IRA units sought weapons in Britain against the wishes of GHQ, who were afraid of affecting the price of weapons available on the black market. Weapons bought by western units were seized by GHQ, further fuelling the tensions within the IRA.

Courtesy of Kilmainham Gaol Museum, 19PC-1B51-04.

Occasionally IRA units in Britain were involved in assassination attempts. The Rochdale Company of the IRA was led by a Straide (MO) man, Ned Ruane, and seemingly dominated by Mayo men. Pictured at his business premises in Rochdale is John Ellis, the hangman who dispatched Republican prisoners hanged by the British. While he was leaving to execute Kevin Barry, the Rochdale Company tried to kill him, but a premature shot spoiled the attempt and his bodyguards managed to get him away.[1] The nature of his work took a heavy toll on Ellis and he later died by his own hand.

Courtesy of Local Studies Centre, Link 4 Life, Arts and Heritage Centre, Rochdale.

1 Seán Walsh, BMH WS 1733, p. 15.

IRA intelligence officers like South Galway's Pádraig Ó Fathaigh (*left*), cultivated a broad range of contacts both within and connected to the crown forces. Among his contacts were two policemen who wrote intelligence reports for British forces, a policeman who was in the personal bodyguard of the local divisional commissioner of the RIC, as well as another regular policeman. Another key informant was Mrs Walshe, a city hotel owner whose establishment was a favoured drinking spot of the Auxiliaries.[1]

On the right is a press photograph of Sir Hugh Jeudwine, OC of the British Army 5th Division. This division's area of operation included Connacht and the picture was found in an IRA intelligence notebook. Other intelligence work included the repeated raiding of mail and the tapping of telephone lines.[2]

In Roscommon written grocery lists provided comparative handwriting samples in the case of two suspected informers, allowing the IRA to identify them.[3] In Roscommon and Leitrim Volunteers dressed like members of the crown forces and visited the homes of suspected informers to see if they would pass information.[4]

Ó Fathaigh courtesy of Finian Ó Fathaigh; Jeudwine courtesy of Irish Military Archives, BMH CD 227/35 (Fintan Murphy Collection).

1 McMahon, *Pádraig Ó Fathaigh's War of Independence*, pp. 82–5.

2 Martin Fallon, BMH WS 1121, p. 21.

3 Thomas Brady, BMH WS 1008, p. 4.

4 *Irish Independent*, 8 April 1921; Report of the First Battalion South Roscommon Brigade February 1921 (P7A/38, Mulcahy Papers, UCD Archives); Patrick Doherty, BMH WS 1195, pp. 29–32.

Although numbers were small in the west, Cumann na mBan carried out invaluable work for the IRA. Pictured is Anne Zita Kelly (née Lynn), a Cumann na mBan intelligence officer in North Mayo. She also taught first aid and carried dispatches and ammunition.[1]

The violence used against women by both sides was usually less severe than that which was used against men. One night in Roscommon the IRA kidnapped a father and daughter who were suspected of informing. The daughter was tied to the railings of a church, the father was shot dead.[2] 'Bobbing' women who were associated with the 'other side' was common and involved the forcible shaving of heads. There are very few reports of sexual assault during that period, but it is difficult to believe, given the vast numbers of men in the various military, guerrilla and police units, that sexual violence didn't occur more frequently than reported. Lady Augusta Gregory, a member of the landed gentry in South Galway, described rumours of sexual assaults carried out by members of the crown forces and a reluctance to report rapes (probably because of a perceived social stigma) in her area.[3]

Courtesy of Kilmainham Gaol Museum, 19MS-1D45-03.

1 Price, *The Flame and the Candle*, p. 49.

2 Monthly Report Third Battalion South Roscommon Brigade May 1921 (P7A/16, Mulcahy Papers, UCD Archives).

3 A. Matthews, *Renegades: Irish Republican Women 1900–1922* (Cork, 2010), pp. 270, 273.

There were different reasons why people informed: ideology, self-protection, personal spite. In one case in Sligo a young woman gave information about the IRA after her boyfriend, an IRA member, broke up with her.[1]

The letter pictured was one of a number intercepted by the IRA in Galway and it led to the shooting of Patrick Joyce, a schoolteacher in Barna (G). One of the factors that drew suspicion onto Joyce was that the letter writer sought to incriminate Martin O'Donnell, who wasn't a member of the IRA but had a legal dispute with Joyce. Joyce was kidnapped, tried by a Republican court, shot and buried. His body remained undiscovered until 1998.[2]

No suspected informers were shot in Mayo, two were shot in Leitrim, one in Sligo and three in Galway. Roscommon saw more executed than the rest of the province, about ten. The reasons for Roscommon's increased use of this type of punishment are unclear and may be related to the attitude towards suspected informers of IRA officers or the pressure being exerted by crown forces. The Roscommon IRA also had several well-placed contacts within the RIC, one of whom at least would have had access to classified information.

It is interesting to note the fact that a large proportion of the suspected informers executed by the IRA were a generation older than the men who shot them. Of the six shot outside Roscommon, at least four were in their fifties or older and a fifth was in his forties. The age profile is harder to establish in Roscommon, but of the suspected informers killed there by the IRA, where age could be established, one was thirty, one was forty and four were in their fifties or sixties.

It should also be noted that an attempt was made by crown forces to pass some of their own killings off as shootings of informers or potential informers by the IRA. This happened, for example, in the cases of Patrick Mulloy shot near Headford (G) and Thomas McEver shot in Dunmore (G).[3]

Courtesy of UCD Archives.

1 Farry, *Sligo 1914–1921*, p. 296.

2 'Body of "informer" shot in 1920 to be reburied', in *Connacht Tribune*, 10 July 1998.

3 C. Ó Comhraí, *Gaillimh 1913–23* (Galway, 2013).

e village of Cappagh one side of the Golf Links is full
Sinnfeiners and all the young men there are
called republican Police. Martin O'Donnell
eing the Captain - with him are the Conneely's
Tom (Junior) - the Lydons. Gannons
McDonaghs. They have sworn vengeance
gainst the Police. Now they are getting up
here into a vacant house. the teacher of
Barna girls School and her husband
that has boasted that he has resigned
from the Police for the love of ~~Ireland~~.
This girls school was the headquarters
of the Sinnfeiners for past two years.
The house in Cappagh is a fine one
able to provide space of from 16 to 20
men and would give troops an
opportunity of killing the volunteers
[illegible] movement there. It is not
wanting by anyone. Captain Waithman has
left it. The warriors in this village
want a bit of fighting. The teacher (Thornton)
of Furbogh is still preaching sedition and
pushing on the young men to shoot

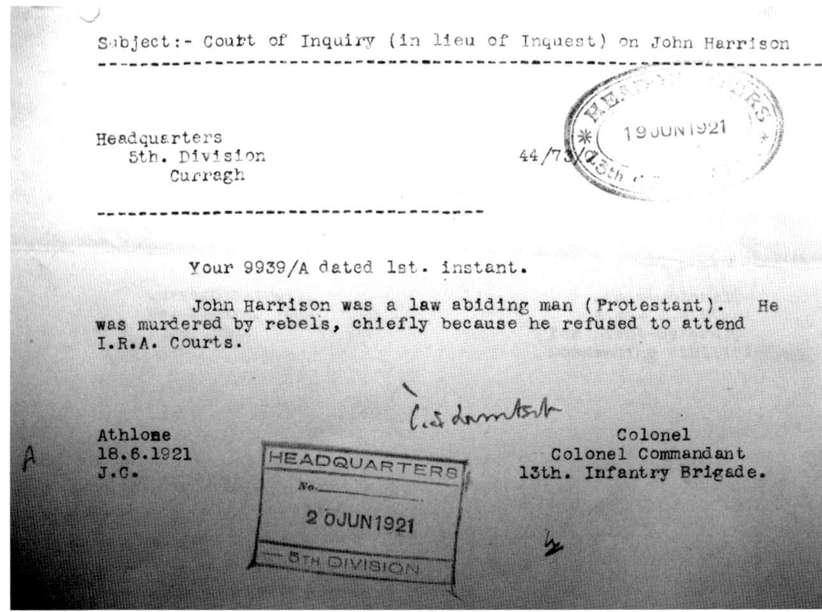

Subject:- Court of Inquiry (in lieu of Inquest) on John Harrison

Headquarters
5th. Division
Curragh

44/73/

19 JUN 1921

Your 9939/A dated 1st. instant.

John Harrison was a law abiding man (Protestant). He was murdered by rebels, chiefly because he refused to attend I.R.A. Courts.

Athlone
18.6.1921
J.C.

Colonel
Colonel Commandant
13th. Infantry Brigade.

HEADQUARTERS
No.
20 JUN 1921
5TH DIVISION

Suspected informers or associates of the crown forces were usually publicly humiliated, beaten or exiled. Punishment was unstructured and depended on the attitude of the local IRA. The campaign against informers was effective. 'I became very ill with the fright I got and since then I have forgotten all about what actually happened in last October' were the words of one Sligo man who had previously passed information to the police.[1] In Sligo and in Leitrim, where there were stronger Protestant communities, the crown forces had some notable successes based on information received from Protestants. The evidence suggests that in the rest of the province, where Protestants were more isolated, they were largely unwilling or unable to pass information. Shortly before suspected informer Thomas Walker was shot in Sligo, he was told: 'If the Protestants were as strong here as in the North/Belfast you'd be bad enough.'[2] The telegram above describes the shooting of John Harrison, a suspected informer from Drumreilly, Ballinamore. According to the crown forces he was: 'A law abiding man (Protestant). He was murdered by rebels, chiefly because he refused to attend I.R.A. Courts.'[3]

Courtesy of the National Archives, Kew, PRO WO 35/151A.

1 Police Report 11 July 1921 in a file on Sligo cases (TNA: PRO CO 904/44).

2 File on murder of Thomas Walker (TNA: PRO CO 904/44).

3 Court of Inquiry (in Lieu of Inquest) on John Harrison (TNA: PRO WO 35/151A).

There was no stereotypical informer and anybody could pass or withhold information. John O'Callaghan, a police informer in Westport (MO), discovered during the Truce that his RIC contact, District Inspector Maguire, was passing information to the IRA. Unsurprisingly O'Callaghan left the area.[1] Constable William Potter, a Protestant RIC man who was killed in Knockcroghery (RN), was an IRA informant.[2]

Even children were mobilised. William Joyce (*pictured seated sixth from the left*), was the son of a loyalist in Galway city. It is probably no surprise that he has been positioned next to the teacher as he was aggressive and fiercely independent. Joyce became a firm favourite of the crown forces and it was suspected by some that he, or his family, assisted crown forces in the killing of Father Griffin in November 1920.[3] Joyce himself claimed later that he had been working with British intelligence.[4] The family left Ireland during the Truce. Joyce became involved with British Fascism before moving onto Nazism. He achieved notoriety because of his propaganda broadcasts from Germany during the Second World War under the name Lord Haw-Haw and was executed by the Allies in 1946.

1 John O'Callaghan (TNA: PRO CO 762/41).

2 Matthew Davis, BMH WS 691, p. 7.

3 See Joseph Togher, BMH WS 1727.

4 J. A. Cole, *Lord Haw-Haw* (London 1964), p. 23.

British intelligence was poor but some British officers displayed a real aptitude for intelligence work, such as District Inspector John Russell in Sligo. Russell had some successes and showed an admirable concern for his informants, continuing to try to secure compensation for losses incurred by them years afterwards.

Pictured is Sligo Republican Linda Kearns. One of Russell's informants gave information that led to her arrest.[1] Kearns was arrested transporting IRA men and arms in a motor car in November 1920 and the British convinced themselves they were all on their way to Dublin to take part in the Bloody Sunday shootings.[2] Kearns escaped over the wall and out of Mountjoy Jail during a prisoners' football match.[3]

Courtesy of Pádraig Óg Ó Ruairc.

In July 1920 the IRA killed Detective William Mulherin, a Mayo man, in Bandon, County Cork. British raids then netted two senior IRA officers who were tortured to the extent that one of them later went insane. Captain Campbell Kelly (*pictured*), the army's senior intelligence officer in Munster, was one of the torturers. The IRA was determined to kill Kelly, although they failed to do so. The intelligence they gathered on him suggested that he was from Kerry or Clare, but it transpires that he was actually from the Ballyhaunis area of County Mayo.[4]

Courtesy of Irish Military Archives, BMH CD 227/35 (Fintan Murphy Collection).

1 George R. Williams (TNA: PRO CO 762/195).

2 TNA: PRO CO 904/44.

3 *IRA Jailbreaks 1918–1921* (Cork 2010), pp. 256–67.

4 For biographical information about Kelly see: http://www.cairogang.com/other-people/british/castle-intelligence/kelly/kelly.html

The increasing danger of capture forced many IRA men to go on the run. Some of the safe houses they stayed in reached legendary status among Republicans for the quality of their hospitality, although it's possible that some of the guests could become a little too comfortable. One of these safe houses in Mayo was described by an IRA man thus:

> There was a great house, Pat Joyce's of Durlis at the back of Croagh Patrick in Drummin … there were no women in the house. Kettrick was in bed one morning and he walked to the door. 'It's a great house,' he said, 'you can have a piss from the door.'[1]

The creation of larger IRA units also led to the use of tents and dugouts, although in isolated areas houses were used. The picture above shows a group of IRA men from the Kinvara area of South Galway.

Extreme left: Bertie Quinn, Pádraig Ó Fathaigh.
Front at table: Seamus Davenport, Joe Kilkelly.
Standing: Tommie Reidy, Tommy Quinn, Mikie Hynes.

Courtesy of Finian Ó Fathaigh.

1 Augusteijn, *From Public Defiance to Guerrilla Warfare*, p. 135.

The numbers of RIC men to combat the IRA were rapidly dwindling as large numbers of men resigned. As a result recruits began arriving from Britain and were nicknamed the Black and Tans because of their ad hoc uniforms. Another force, the Auxiliaries, was recruited among ex-British military officers. The photograph above is from an IRA intelligence notebook showing the Auxiliaries based at Lenaboy Castle, Galway city.

Courtesy of Irish Military Archives, BMH CD 227/35 (Fintan Murphy Collection).

The new policemen had no shortage of friends. In East Mayo: 'The Tans walked out with the best-looking girls from Kiltimagh.'[1] Their behaviour was less than ideal, however. One policeman recorded:

> Black and Tans in Roscommon did not confine themselves to the looting of Jackson's shop for jewellery, blankets and other articles of wearing apparel. It was a common practice for them when they went out the country in their lorries to shoot down fowl and other poultry, the property of poor people, and bring them back to the mess ...'[2]

Docile native policemen were sidelined or retired, amongst them District Inspector Thomas Flanagan (*left*) from Elphin (RN), who was apparently blamed for the stand-off between the men under his command and his superiors in Listowel, Kerry, in June 1920.[3]

Courtesy J. Anthony Gaughan.

---

1 Interview with Tom Carney (P17b/109, O'Malley Notebooks, UCD Archives).

2 John Duffy, BMH WS 580, p. 23.

3 Gaughan, *The Memoirs of Constable Jeremiah Mee*, p. 152.

Relations between old and new RIC men were often strained. Sergeant Thomas Browne (he was promoted to sergeant in 1920) was stationed at Oranmore (G) during the War of Independence. In the summer of 1920 he was twice shot and wounded by members of the IRA. However, family folklore also recalls that he was wounded by a Black and Tan for helping a local escape their attention through emigration.

Courtesy of Paul Browne.

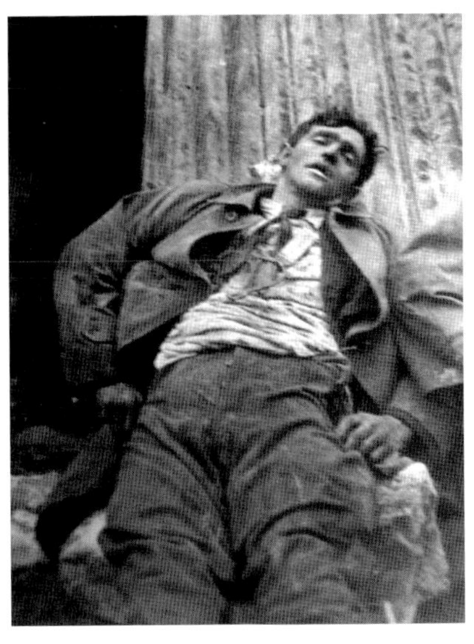

Pictured is an unidentified victim of an ambush in the west of Ireland. Major ambushes carried out by the IRA against the crown forces began to occur in the west in the summer and autumn of 1920. It was fear of these ambushes and the impact of seeing dead colleagues that triggered many of the major British reprisals, such as the one at Tubbercurry (SO) in the autumn of 1920. After the Carrowkennedy (MO) ambush in June 1921 the desire to inflict revenge was thought to have been diluted by the positive treatment received by captured and wounded members of the RIC.[1] Not all violence occurred in the immediate aftermath of ambushes, however, and some was simply inexplicable.

Courtesy of the National Archives, Kew, PRO CO 904/121.

1 Augusteijn, *From Public Defiance to Guerrilla Warfare*, p. 240.

This picture shows Cliffony Barracks in Sligo during the War of Independence, with members of the crown forces outside. On 25 October 1920 four RIC men from the barracks were killed in an ambush led by Billy Pilkington, Sligo Brigade commandant. All four RIC were Irishmen and one, Patrick Laffey, was a Galway man. On 27 June 1921 Constable Patrick Clarke, a Mayo man, left this barracks and was shot dead by the IRA.[1] Note the efforts made to protect the entrance to the barracks with sandbags.

Barbed wire was also frequently used to slow any attempt to rush a barracks door. Sergeant Francis Butler, a Roscommon man stationed at Newport (MO), who had a reputation for brutality, was shot dead by a sniper as he picked his way through 'a maze of barbed wire defences at the front of the barracks.'[2]

Courtesy of Bedfordshire and Luton Archives Service X550-2-6_p96a.

1 R. Abbott, *Police Casualties in Ireland* (Cork, 2000), pp. 139, 259.

2 *Ibid.*, p. 244; Price, *The Flame and the Candle*, p. 144.

In a reprisal for the actions of the IRA in Cliffony the Sinn Féin hall in the town was burned by British forces, who made the reason for their actions clear to passers-by.

Courtesy of Bedfordshire and Luton Archives Service X550-2-6_p133.

A substantial number of policemen actively helped the revolution. Head Constable Peter Folan (*left*), a Spiddal (G) man working in Dublin Castle, passed information to the IRA.[1] Constable Bernard Conway of Cliffony (SO) (*top left*), and Constable Thomas Hargaden (LM) (*top right*), assisted the IRA in capturing Cookstown RIC Barracks in Tyrone in June 1920, leading to a significant haul of arms for the rebels.[2]

Photographs courtesy of Enda Folan and J. Anthony Gaughan.

1 Peter Folan, BMH WS 316.

2 For an examination of Conway and Hargaden see Gaughan, *The Memoirs of Constable Jeremiah Mee.*

While some clergymen gave open or tacit support to the Republican campaign, others remained steadfastly hostile and sought to prevent IRA activity. Archbishop Thomas Gilmartin of Tuam, originally from Ballyvary (MO), became the object of hostility among western Republicans because of his efforts to prevent the IRA acting in his diocese. After the Gallagh ambush (G) on 19 July 1920, when two members of the RIC were killed by the IRA and a large part of Tuam burned by crown forces, Gilmartin declared a 'Truce of God' in his diocese. He described the IRA men who ambushed Auxiliaries in Kilroe, Headford (G), as guilty of murder[1] and summoned Petie McDonnell, OC West Connemara Brigade IRA, to try to dissuade him from founding a flying column in West Connemara.[2]

Courtesy of Tuam Diocesan Archives.

1 P. Murray, *Oracles of God: The Roman Catholic Church and Irish Politics, 1922–37* (Dublin, 2000), p. 409.

2 Ó Comhraí, *Gaillimh 1913–23*.

People who were felt to have behaved treacherously towards the crown forces were targeted during reprisals. Pictured is the home of former Constable Bernard Conway at Cliffony (SO), which was burned by members of the crown forces. Conway, whose brother Andrew was an active IRA man, may well have been suspected of complicity in the Cookstown Barracks raid, as the British realised that the IRA had received help from inside the barracks.

Protestants who held Republican and nationalist sympathies or who criticised the crown forces were targeted on occasion by those forces. It is possible that their religious background was a factor in identifying them as targets in some cases. James Monds, a Protestant land agitator with Republican sympathies from Knockmurry, Castlerea (RN), was taken from his home and shot dead by members of the crown forces on 6 April 1921.[1]

Courtesy of J. Anthony Gaughan.

1 Hegarty Thorne, *They Put the Flag a-Flyin'*, p. 386.

On 21 August 1920 members of the Castlegar (G) Company of the IRA ambushed a police patrol at Merlin Park and Constable Martin Foley (*left*), a Roscommon man, was killed. Over the following months eight locals, none of whom participated in the ambush, were shot by members of the police, with one, Joe Athy, dying. During the course of the reprisals Keane's pub (*above*) was burned down. Joe Howley, Mrs Keane's son from a previous marriage, although a leading IRA man, was wrongly blamed for the ambush.

Image of pub courtesy of Pádraig Keane; image of Foley courtesy of Kate Foley.

Not all police violence was the work of British Black and Tans and Auxiliaries. Some native RIC men, like Head Constable Eugene Igoe of Attymass (MO) (*pictured*), quickly gained promotion despite, or perhaps because of, their willingness to flout the law. A special unit was created and led by Igoe in Dublin to patrol the streets looking for rural Volunteers visiting IRA headquarters.

Courtesy of Kilmainham Gaol Museum, 19PO-1A32-03.

The first victim of Igoe's unit was Joe Howley (*pictured*), who was killed at Broadstone Railway Station in December 1920. When Howley and Paddy Mullins, a Ballyhaunis (MO) medical student involved with the Galway IRA, alighted from the train they were fired at from close range. Howley was shot in the head and died soon afterwards. Mullins escaped into the crowd and disappeared.[1]

An attempt to use a Castlegar (G) Volunteer, Thomas 'Sweeney' Newell, to identify Igoe and perhaps ensnare him, led to Newell being seriously wounded and tortured by Igoe. However, Igoe was also capable of acts of decency, even to Newell, whose life he spared.[2] On another occasion, meeting a Mayo Sinn Féiner who was on the run from death threats in Galway, Igoe pretended not to recognise him, remembering that the Republican had treated his father decently.[3]

Image courtesy of Pádraig Keane.

1 Martin Dolan, 'Galway 1920–1921' in *Capuchin Annual* 1970, pp. 384–95; *The Freeman's Journal,* 6 December 1920.

2 Thomas 'Sweeney' Newell, BMH WS 698, pp. 4–7.

3 Patrick Moylett, BMH WS 767, p. 48.

The railways were a key component of the IRA's ability to move men, materials and intelligence. In Galway city the IRA had two important railway contacts, both Roscommon men.

On 8 September 1920 Galway city IRA man Seán Turke (*left*) was in charge of a small group of IRA men awaiting arms to be delivered on the Dublin train. A drunken Black and Tan, Constable Edward Krumm, blundered into the station. During an altercation the IRA attempted to disarm Krumm and Volunteer Seán (Jack) Mulvoy and Krumm were both shot dead. That night Lieutenant Séamus Quirke was taken from his lodgings and shot dead by the police during a police riot. It was thought that the police confused the names Quirke and Turke.

It is likely that the police rioters were drinking and although they tried to kill IRA commandant Johnny Broderick (*right*) and another Volunteer, they botched both attempts. An attempt was also made to set fire to Broderick's home on the same evening and people who tried to fight the flames had shots fired over their heads.

One of the IRA's contacts at Galway Railway Station, Hugh (Hubert) Tully from Clooneyquinn (RN), was shot dead in his lodgings on 11 May 1921.[1]

Courtesy of Mellows Barracks.

1 Patrick Moylett, BMH WS 767, p. 32; *Connacht Tribune*, 11 September 1920 and 14 May 1921; *Evidence on Conditions in Ireland* (Washington 1921), pp. 84–5, 133, 410–413, 852–854; Seán Broderick, BMH WS 1677, pp. 5–6.

On 30 September 1920 the IRA ambushed a police lorry at Chaffpool near Tubbercurry (SO), killing District Inspector James Joseph Brady. That night saw large numbers of policemen and military involved in burnings, which were accompanied by the sounds of gunfire and a looted melodeon. The family of District Inspector Brady publicly condemned the burnings.[1] Pictured is the barracks of the Auxiliaries in Tubbercurry – note the destroyed buildings in the background.

Courtesy of Bedfordshire and Luton Archives Service X550-2-6-p52a.

1 Farry, *Sligo 1914–1921*.

Pictured are the survivors of an IRA attack on Kilmallock Barracks that was carried out in May 1920. By 1921 Tobias O'Sullivan (*centre*), a sergeant at the time of the attack in Limerick, was a district inspector. A native of the Cornamona area of North Galway, O'Sullivan was shot dead while in the company of his young son in January 1921 in Listowel, Kerry, because of his ability to identify a Republican prisoner, the leader of the Kilmallock attack, who was in danger of being executed if identified.[1] By coincidence another Galway RIC man, Constable Edward Daly from the Tuam area, helped the IRA capture Schull RIC Barracks in Cork by supplying them with the password, 'Kilmallock'.[2]

Courtesy of Getty Images.

1 T. Toomey, *The War of Independence in Limerick 1912–1921* (Limerick, 2010), pp. 506–8.

2 Liam Deasy, 'The Schull Peninsula in the War of Independence' in *Éire-Ireland* (Summer 1966), pp. 5–18.

Angered by reports of British excesses in Ireland, members of the Connaught Rangers Regiment serving in India mutinied. Fearful of the mutiny spreading to other units, the military leadership sentenced the mutineers to long sentences and one, James Daly (*right*), was executed. Daly described himself and is often described as 'of Tyrell's Pass, County Westmeath', but he was actually born in North Galway and spent much of his childhood and youth there. Pictured above are a group of Connaught Rangers at a later commemoration of the mutiny.

Courtesy of Kilmainham Gaol Museum, 19PO-3N12-202 and 1PO-1A36-21.

Frustrated at their inability to catch the most active Republicans, members of the crown forces often took that frustration out on family members. John Reilly, the teenage brother of IRA man Michael Reilly from Kilbeacanty, Gort (G), was taken down this country lane in 1921 by members of the crown forces, blindfolded and subjected to a mock execution.[1]

Thomas Brady of Drinane, Strokestown (RN), was an active member of the North Roscommon Brigade. During a crown forces raid on the family's house, Thomas feigned sickness. When his father pointed out that Thomas's brother was an ex-soldier, the crown forces left. Clearly discovering that they had been tricked, they returned to find that Thomas had disappeared. His father was beaten up and threatened. Thomas later wrote: 'Our house was raided practically every week after that and my father was subject to abuse by beating and putting revolvers to his head and telling him he was going to die and so forth. He was then almost eighty years old.'[2]

Author's collection.

1 Information courtesy of John Reilly junior.

2 Thomas Brady, BMH WS 1008, p. 9.

Donnelly's Pub in Barna (G). Racism was a factor in the behaviour of British forces, often manifesting itself in a violent response to anything Gaelic. The owners of this pub were threatened with death in October 1920 because of their refusal to remove the Irish-language version of the pub's name.[1] The pub was bombed by members of the crown forces in November 1920.[2]

While it was logical to assume that commitment to the Irish language revival signalled militant nationalist tendencies, this was often not the case. Some Republicans had little or no interest in the language and some committed Unionists and servants of the state did. For example, John Gaughan, an RIC man from Mayo who was shot dead in Carlow in 1920, had been an Irish teacher before joining the force.[3]

Courtesy of Joe O'Connor.

1 W. Henry, *Blood for Blood: The Black and Tan War in Galway* (Cork, 2012), p. 125.

2 *Connacht Tribune*, 27 November 1920.

3 Abbott, *Police Casualties in Ireland*, p. 119.

Little effort seems to have been made to punish those members of crown forces responsible for the violence. Some senior officers, such as General Hugh Tudor, chief of police in Ireland 1920–21, and senior government politicians, such as Sir Hamar Greenwood (*above*), effectively gave the crown forces carte blanche to do as they pleased. On 2 November 1920 Ellen Quinn, a pregnant woman with a child on her lap, was shot and fatally wounded at Kiltartan (G) by a member of the crown forces in a passing lorry. IPP MP Joe Devlin raised her death in the House of Commons, eliciting the following discussion:

> Sir Hamar Greenwood replied, 'I am informed by the police authorities that two police lorries were passing, and it may be that the firing took place in anticipation of an ambush in the neighbourhood.'
>
> 'From a baby in arms?' interjected Mr Devlin.
>
> ... the Chief Secretary (Greenwood) said that of course, there was a very careful record kept of the patrols, the time of their departure, route and return and the amount of ammunition expended. In Ireland and especially in Galway he added, amid Coalition cheers, the police and military had every right to anticipate ambushes ...[1]

Courtesy of Kilmainham Gaol Museum, 19PC-1A54-01.

1 *Irish Independent*, 5 November 1920.

Increased IRA activity led to the deployment of additional troops to the area. Pictured are a unit of the 17th Lancers Regiment of the British Army at Earl's Island beside the university in Galway, May 1921.

Garrisoned in large, well-armed units, and with few having a role in the intelligence conflict, British soldiers were rarely attacked in the west of Ireland during the War of Independence. While individual RIC men became defined as 'good' or 'bad', it was army regiments, rather than individual soldiers, that became so defined. For example, the 6th Dragoon Guards, who were garrisoned in Earl's Island before the Lancers, had a reputation for wanton brutality.[1] In Leitrim it was alleged that members of the Bedfordshire Regiment killed two wounded IRA men by crushing their skulls with rifle butts.[2] As occurred in the ranks of the RIC, Republican attacks could lead to a loss or abandonment of discipline. After an ambush at Scramogue (RN), during which they lost at least two officers, the 9th Queen's Royal Lancers were in an ugly mood, which put suspected Republicans in their custody in very real danger. Ironically, given their reputation, it was Black and Tans who protected the Republican prisoners.[3]

Courtesy of the Queen's Royal Lancers Museum.

1 Ó Comhraí, *Gaillimh 1913–23.*

2 Ernie O'Malley, *Raids and Rallies* (Cork, 2011), p. 136.

3 Patrick Mullooly, BMH WS 955, p. 23.

The Argyll and Sutherland Highlanders Regiment stationed in Claremorris (MO) and Galway was well respected. Their commanding officer, Lieutenant Colonel W. J. B. Tweedie, gave the lead, and the regiment collectively demonstrated a strong sense of right and wrong.[1]

Courtesy of the Argyll and Sutherland Highlanders Regiment Museum.

In Galway city Sergeant Pat Margetts, an Englishman in the Highlanders, began to pass information to people who he felt were in danger from the crown forces. In the autumn of 1920 forty or fifty soldiers, seemingly from the same regiment, held a protest march in Galway city and publicly threatened to retaliate against the Auxiliaries if violence against civilians continued.[2]

Courtesy of the Margetts family.

1 O'Malley and Ó Comhraí, *The Men will Talk to Me*, pp. 278–80.

2 *Roscommon Herald,* 2 October 1920.

Pictured are prisoners exercising in Boyle Military Barracks, where they were held before transfer to internment camps. From the winter of 1920–21 the British government started using internment without trial. Thousands of suspected Republicans were arrested. Interrogations by army intelligence officers and RIC men were often brutal. Con Fogarty, OC Tuam Brigade IRA, later wrote:

> I was interrogated by two Black and Tans named Pinkie and Anderson about the ambush. I was told I was to be shot. I was handed a rosary beads and a lighted candle. I was beaten about the head and again questioned, but I refused to talk. I was given half an hour to consider whether I would die or give information. I was taken out again and put against a wall, and shots fired. I was again beaten and questioned, still I refused to talk.[1]

Even under arrest some refused to be cowed. James Nohilly from Tuam (G) told his interrogators:

> I consider that the only true patriots in Ireland are the Sinn Féin members of Parliament. I am a strong adherent of the IRA and I shall continue to lend them all the assistance in my power and to take an active part in the movement until Ireland has gained her Freedom.[2]

Courtesy of Bedfordshire and Luton Archives Service X550-2-6_p111a.

1 Michael (Con) Fogarty, BMH WS 673, p. 11.

2 Suspects implicated in Kilroe ambush, Tuam (TNA: PRO WO 35/129).

Suspected IRA men were sent to camps in the Curragh (Kildare) and Ballykinlar, County Down (*above*). Inevitably mistakes were made. Boyle (RN) Republican James Feely was interned without the opportunity being taken to question him about his activities.[1] Some were imprisoned on spurious grounds. William Reilly from Headford (G) was interned for 'possession of copybook in which seditious songs were written'.[2] Others, such as Ballina (MO) Republican John Moran, were released because of influential friends, in Moran's case the Bishop of Killala.[3] Joe Togher (*left*), a key IRA intelligence officer in Galway city, bluffed successfully about his role in the IRA and was released.[4]

Ballykinlar courtesy of Kilmainham Gaol Museum, 19PO-1A32-07; Togher courtesy of Mellows Barracks.

1 James Feely, BMH WS 997, p. 10.
2 Courts Martial (TNA: PRO WO 35/130).
3 John Moran, BMH WS 1549, p. 5.
4 Joseph Togher, BMH WS 1727.

Republicans violated both Protestant and Catholic religious practices by using churches to mount attacks from and house wanted men, weapons or their own prisoners. The behaviour of members of the crown forces was even worse. Contempt towards Catholic religious sensitivities and clergymen, as well as allegations of bias in the manner in which sectarian trouble in the north-east was handled, were widely reported in the press. Funerals such as that of John O'Hanlon (*right*), a Republican from Lackagh (G) who was shot dead by crown forces, were attacked. Vestments, religious icons and pictures were vandalised. Catholic priests who criticised the crown forces or were overtly Republican were targeted, with one, Father Michael Griffin, being lured from his home, shot by members of the crown forces and buried in Barna (G) in November 1920. The above monument was erected to his memory at the spot.

O'Hanlon courtesy of Gerry O'Hanlon; Griffin monument courtesy of Joe O'Connor.

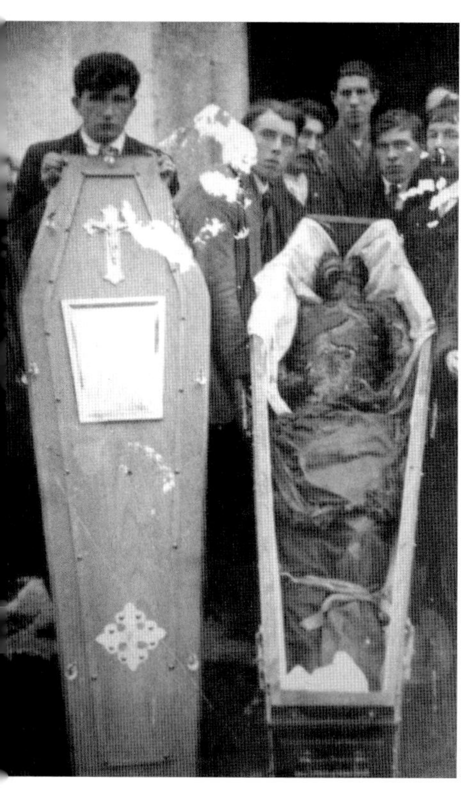

Pictured are the bodies of Pat and Harry Loughnane, Shanaglish (G). They were arrested by Auxiliaries and tortured to death, almost certainly by being dragged behind a lorry. An attempt was made to burn their bodies before they were finally dumped in a pond.[1] The terror caused by killings such as these had an effect. Towards the end of 1920 and early in 1921 independent efforts were made by several groups and individuals to bring about peace. Patrick Moylett (a Mayo businessman), a small group of councillors from Galway County Council and Father Michael O'Flanagan were among those involved.[2] These efforts ultimately failed, but they encouraged the British to continue coercion and, by giving the British the idea that the Republican cause was close to collapse, frustrated the feelers that the British and the Republican movement were sending in each other's direction.

Courtesy of Irish Military Archives, BMH P39.

1 O'Malley, and Ó Comhraí, *The Men will Talk to Me*, pp. 286–90.

2 Hopkinson, *The Irish War of Independence*, pp. 180–3.

Active IRA men in inactive areas often migrated to more active ones and these IRA men were welcomed into their new units. Pictured are four men from South Galway who joined the Mid-Clare flying column early in 1921. The women are unidentified. The men are: standing (*left to right*): Mikie Hynes and Seamus Davenport; seated (*left to right*): Pádraig Ó Fathaigh and Pádraig Kilkelly.

Courtesy of Finian Ó Fathaigh.

Republicans provided reliable, if selective, information to the world's press which was often trusted more than government information. Alienated from the press, British forces attacked both *The Galway Express* and the *Leitrim Observer.*[1] Geraldine Plunkett Dillon (*right*), who was living in Galway city during this period, spent a month in jail having been caught with accounts of beatings received by Republican suspects in Eglinton Street Barracks (G). During the raid her daughter was told that they would shoot her mother, soiled sanitation towels and underwear were used 'as decorations' and Irish language books were burned.[2]

Courtesy of Honor Ó Brolchain.

The propaganda campaign had a major impact on Irish-Americans. James Brendan Connolly (*left*), who became the first Olympic champion of the modern era in 1896 when he won the first event, the triple jump, was the son of emigrants from the Aran Islands (G). He was appointed Commissioner for the American Committee for Relief in Ireland. The committee was set up to assist financially civilians who had suffered hardship as a result of the War of Independence.

Courtesy of Colby College, Maine.

1 I. Kenneally, *The Paper Wall: Newspapers and Propaganda in Ireland 1919–1921* (Cork, 2008), p. 16.

2 G. Plunkett Dillon, *All in the Blood* (Dublin, 2006), p. 303.

Towards the end of 1920 the IRA established divisions, comprising several brigades, in an effort to increase activity and take the pressure off the more active areas. South Galway and all of Clare were put into the 1st Western Division, which was established in the spring of 1921 under the leadership of Michael Brennan, OC of the East Clare Brigade. His intelligence officer was Séamus Hogan (*pictured*) from Kilreecle (G) and he became divisional intelligence officer. Brennan travelled into South Galway, met local IRA men and established the South-West and South-East Galway Brigades. IRA officers who were thought to be aggressive were promoted over the heads of more cautious activists and the new brigades were supported with the transfer to the area of experienced Claremen to provide them with assistance.

Hogan later served as Professor of History at University College Cork for forty years.

Courtesy of University College Cork.

From the spring of 1921 the IRA in the west began using full-time columns of men who were on the run, known as flying columns. There could be anything from ten to forty men in one of these columns. Few attacks occurred in towns and they supplied few active guerrillas. Republicans looked down on townspeople because of their perceived failure to contribute: 'Newport [MO] town was never any good.'[1] There was also occasionally tension between the men of the columns and the non-column Volunteers who were left behind, unarmed, to bear the brunt of British reprisals.[2] Pictured is a column in the Mid-Galway Brigade area.

Front from left: Thomas 'Baby' Duggan (Castlegar), Christy Courtney (Athenry), Brian Molloy (Castlegar) and Martin Gannon.

Standing: Pádraic Feeney (Claregalway), John Tynan, Patrick Glynn (Headford) and Michael Cunningham.

Courtesy of Finian Ó Fathaigh.

1 Michael Kilroy interview (P17b/101, O'Malley notebooks, UCD Archives).

2 Augusteijn, *From Public Defiance to Guerrilla Warfare*, p. 162.

Pictured are Paddy Moran (*left*) from Crossna (RN) and Tommy Whelan (*right*) from Clifden (G). The photograph was taken shortly before they were executed in Dublin in March 1921 for their alleged part in the shooting of suspected British intelligence operatives in November 1920 on Bloody Sunday. Both men were innocent of the charges they were convicted for, but only technically in the case of Moran as he was involved in another shooting on that day.[1] Whelan was a Volunteer, but inactive. He met his death bravely, telling a cell mate: 'I can hardly call myself a soldier as I never fired a shot, but perhaps I can save a good soldier's life.'[2] Also pictured is a box of chocolates that Whelan was to share with the child of his landlady in the event of his release, but that she was to eat in the event of his execution. Despite his execution the chocolates were never eaten.

Courtesy of Kilmainham Gaol Museum, 19PO-1A33-22 (h) and 19EF-3F11-03.

1 Foy, *Michael Collins's Intelligence War*, pp. 171–2; Moran, *Executed for Ireland*.

2 Maj.-General Patrick O'Daly statement, pp. 52–3 (National Library P4548).

Whenever executions were carried out, large crowds of supporters gathered outside the prison. Pictured here is Thomas Whelan's mother, Bridget, outside Mountjoy Jail in a traditional west of Ireland shawl. Republican Geraldine Plunkett Dillon later wrote about Whelan's last hours: 'Tom Whelan's mother was allowed to see him before he was hanged and he sang for her in the condemned cell her favourite song, "The Shawl of Galway Grey".'[1]

Courtesy of Getty Images.

1 Plunkett Dillon, *All in the Blood*, p. 302.

Members of the British Army and a member of the RIC pictured early in 1921 at Keadue (RN). Following the executions of Moran and Whelan the IRA attacked police patrols in their home areas. At Keadue (RN) the police were lured into an ambush through a raid on a post office. Two policemen were shot dead and a third wounded when a patrol was sent to investigate the incident.[1] In Clifden (G) a newly formed flying column led by Petie McDonnell entered the town, attacked a police patrol and sniped the barracks to prevent reinforcements arriving. Two policemen were shot dead, which led to widespread burnings by British forces during which they shot an ex-British Army soldier dead.[2]

Courtesy of Bedfordshire and Luton Archives Service X550-2-6_p52a.

1 Hegarty Thorne, *They Put the Flag a-Flyin'*, pp. 83–4.

2 O'Malley and Ó Comhraí, *The Men Will Talk to Me*, p. 296.

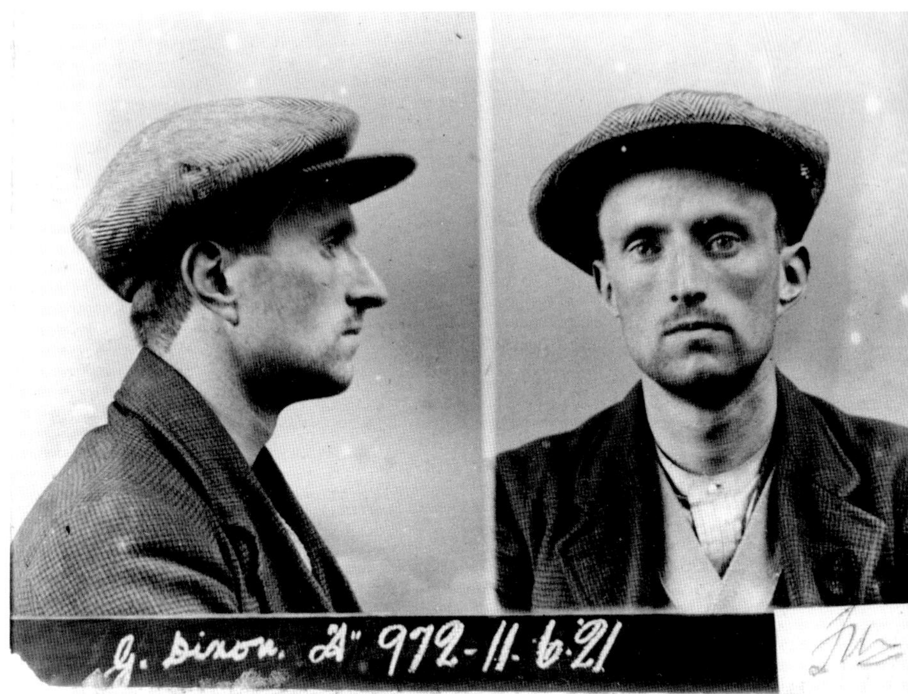

The IRA's organisers, who were sent from IRA GHQ to increase levels of activities in provincial units, paid a heavy price for their involvement, with several being killed. For example, Louis D'Arcy, a medical student in UCD, was sent to Headford (G), his home area. While returning to the area from a trip to IRA GHQ, D'Arcy was taken from the train at Oranmore by the RIC or Auxiliaries and later shot. Either he was dragged behind a lorry before being shot, or his body was dragged afterwards.[1]

'G. Dixon' (*pictured*) was luckier. That was the alias used by Gerald Davis, a Kilgefin (RN) man also studying in Dublin, who was sent to Athlone. He was arrested after an attack on two RIC men close to Athlone and sent to Mountjoy Jail.[2]

Courtesy of the National Archives of Ireland, D/Justice, Mountjoy Jail-2011/124/2/64.

1 Thomas Hynes, BMH WS 714, p. 15; Plunkett Dillon, *All in the Blood*, p. 303.

2 Gerald Davis, BMH WS 1361, pp. 12–15.

On 4 March the military were lured into an ambush by a bogus informer's letter which told them that wanted men would be at a church in Gowel (LM). On their return to Carrick-on-Shannon they were ambushed and one soldier was killed.[1] A week later, after receiving information from William Latimer, a local farmer, and Doctor Charles Pentland, the crown forces had their revenge. The IRA column responsible for the ambush was surrounded at Selton Hill (LM) by soldiers guided by District Inspector Thomas Gore-Hickman (*above*). Several of the IRA men escaped, but six members of the column were killed. Another, Bernie Sweeney, escaped, despite being seriously wounded, by lying in a drain where he remained undetected. In retaliation for informing, Latimer was later shot dead, although Pentland escaped to London. He died there, having been crushed by a lorry.[2] Property belonging to Gore-Hickman was later burned to the ground by the IRA in Clare.[3]

Courtesy of Irish Military Archives, BMH CD 227/35 (Fintan Murphy Collection).

1 List of Outrages (TNA: PRO WO 35/89).

2 Patrick Joseph Hargaden, BMH WS 1268, p. 14; Charles Pinkman, BMH WS 1263, pp. 7–10; Eugene Kilkenny, BMH WS 1146, p. 12.

3 P. Óg Ó Ruairc, *Revolution: A Photographic History of Revolutionary Ireland* (Cork, 2011), p. 145.

The six members of the column who were killed at Selton Hill. Clockwise, starting top left: Seamus Wrynn, John Joe O'Reilly, Michael Baxter, Seán Connolly, Joe Beirne, John Joe O'Reilly.

Courtesy of Michael Whelan.

Motivated by a desire to avenge the death of Seán Connolly, who had spent some time with the IRA in Roscommon, the IRA attacked a lorry of the 9th Queen's Royal Lancers in Scramogue. Lieutenant Roger Granville Peek (*pictured*) and at least one other soldier were killed. Two Black and Tans who were being transported as prisoners were also killed by the IRA after they had taken these men with them in the mistaken belief that they were Republican prisoners. A number of ex-soldiers played a key role in the IRA attack.[1]

Copyright of the 9th/12th Lancers Museum.

Above is an image of Peek's funeral in England.

Copyright of the 9th/12th Lancers Museum.

1 O'Malley, *Raids and Rallies*, pp. 139–58.

Patrick Pearse's cottage in Rosmuck (G). The house was burned by British forces after an ambush at nearby Screebe on 6 April 1921, where a Constable William Pearson from New Zealand was fatally wounded in an attack carried out by the West Connemara Brigade, IRA.[1] The photograph shows the house after it had been rebuilt in the 1920s.

The same night a local co-operative was burned by crown forces. That attempt at collective, economic punishment during reprisals was not an isolated phenomenon. A number of creameries were destroyed in Sligo: Rathscanlon, Ballymote, Curry, Achonry and Ballintrillick.[2]

Courtesy of the Pearse Museum, Dublin.

1 O'Malley and Ó Comhraí, *The Men Will Talk to Me*, pp. 124–5.

2 Farry, *Sligo 1914–1921*.

IRA flying columns proved capable of engaging and then withdrawing successfully from large numbers of British forces. On 3 May the South Mayo Brigade, IRA flying column (*above*) killed five members of the RIC during an attack on Tourmakeady (MO). Despite the shooting dead of their adjutant, Michael O'Brien (*right*), and the wounding of their commandant, Tom Maguire, the column avoided capture.

The column members in the photograph are:

Back row (*left to right*): Mattie Flannery, Tommy Fahy (both Ballinrobe), Jack and Mick Collins (Cong), John Butler, Terry O'Brien, Martin Conroy and Tom Lally (all Ballinrobe).

Front row: Tom Maguire (Cross, *standing*), Paddy King (Tourmakeady), Tommy Cavannagh (Cross), Seamus Burke (The Neale), Michael Shaughnessy and Michael Corless (Cross), Lt Seamus O'Brien (Kilmaine), Tommy Carney (Cong), Paddy Gibbons (Tourmakeady), Tom Murphy (Cong) and Paddy Maye (Ballinrobe, *standing to the right*).

Reclining front: Michael 'Soldier' Costello (Tourmakeady) and Jack Ferguson (Ballinrobe – originally from Leitrim).

Courtesy of James Dooley.

Joe Stanford, seated left, became OC of the South-West Galway Brigade during IRA reorganisation in April 1921. Pat Glynn, also seated, became vice-commandant of Gort Battalion and Dan Ryan, standing, became brigade quartermaster.

Courtesy of the Stanford family.

British forces arrested Michael Dockery, OC of the North Roscommon Brigade IRA, in May 1921. Caught with a rifle taken at a fatal ambush it looked likely that he would be executed. With the help of a British soldier, Dockery escaped from Boyle Barracks (*above*). Apparently the soldier helped him escape because he had been in a prison camp himself during the First World War.[1] Dockery later joined the Free State Army and was killed in Boyle in July 1922, at the start of the Civil War.[2]

Courtesy of Bedfordshire and Luton Archives Service X550-2-6_66a.

1 Andrew Keaveney, BMH WS 1178, p. 11.

2 Hegarty Thorne, *They Put the Flag a-Flyin'*, p. 261.

On 15 May 1921 the South-West Galway Brigade ambushed District Inspector Cecil Blake (*left*), a recent English recruit to the RIC, his wife and their companions as they drove from Ballyturin House, near Gort (G). Captain Cornwallis had left their car to open a gate when 'Hands up' was called. Fire was opened but it's unclear who fired first, Cornwallis or the IRA.

Fire was directed at the car whose passengers scrambled to get out. A member of the local gentry, Margaret Gregory, was the only survivor. The ambush was portrayed as cold-blooded murder by its critics and to a lesser degree by Margaret Gregory. On the other hand, Republicans and an initial press report created an image of Lily Blake (*below*) refusing to leave her husband's side and dying with him, as well as Margaret Gregory being spared. More likely than either scenario, perhaps, is that inexperienced Volunteers fired at a flurry of movement coming out of the car when they heard the initial shots and that Margaret Gregory, who seems to have exited the car on the other side to her companions, was fortunate rather than deliberately spared during an ambush that was going according to plan.

Later, RIC man Constable John Kearney from Abbeydorney, Kerry, was shot dead at the site of the ambush by his fellow policemen. He had been passing intelligence reports to the IRA.[1]

Cecil Blake courtesy of Paul Blake; Lily Blake courtesy of Emma Gilmour.

1 Ó Comhraí, *Gaillimh 1913–23*.

Extensive reprisals followed the Ballyturin ambush, including the burning of the home of Pádraig Ó Fathaigh (*above*). The same weekend the family buried Máire, Pádraig's sister, and her funeral was attacked by members of the crown forces.[1]

Courtesy of Finian Ó Fathaigh.

Increased Republican activity led to a decrease in reprisals in some areas, but some members of the crown forces became even more erratic. In June 1921 the village of Knockcroghery (RN) (*pictured*) was burned by members of the crown forces. To this day the precise motive remains unclear.[2]

Courtesy of Frank Beattie.

1 McMahon, *Pádraig Ó Fathaigh's War of Independence*.

2 Hegarty Thorne, *They Put the Flag a-Flyin'*, pp. 104–5.

Increased disruption to the road network hampered the mobility of the crown forces and steered them towards ambush sites, as happened at the Carrowkennedy ambush in Mayo. Where the IRA had high explosives and engineers proficient in their use these were used effectively. These pictures show bridges destroyed at Grange (SO), and near Ballymote (SO) (*inset*). The attack on infrastructure was not without opponents. One member of the West Connemara Brigade, IRA, wrote:

> We went to Cornamona to destroy a bridge ... Father O'Grady would not listen ... he would stand on the bridge and let it be blown up under his feet. To this Father Tracey said: 'Good-bye, John! See you in Heaven ... maybe!' With that, the C.O. gave the order to clear the bridge and take cover. Father O'Grady was not too far away when the explosion shook the countryside and split the bridge in two.

The incident had unexpected consequences:

> There was an old man named Lowery who would not get out of his house, as he was suffering from severe rheumatism. He was lifted from his bed by the concussion, and when he got to his feet, his old bones had become limber as a child's. I heard that he became an ardent Republican.[1]

Courtesy of Bedfordshire and Luton Archives Service X550-2-6_137a and X550-2-6_p47a.

1 John C. King, BMH WS 1731, p. 14.

Trenching was another tactic adopted by the IRA to obstruct military lorries, but they were careful to try and leave room for local carts. Note the manner in which this road is only partially trenched.

Civilians were often compelled by British forces to refill roads (*as above*), an act which further alienated them from the crown forces.

It was dangerous to be caught trenching roads. On 19 May 1921 members of the RIC came upon a group of IRA men trenching the Castlebar/Westport road at Clonkeen. Two were arrested and cousins Thomas O'Malley and Thomas Lally were shot dead.[1]

In Roscommon four men were wounded on the Lanesboro/Roscommon road when British forces booby-trapped a road targeting those who might retrench it.[2]

Courtesy of Bedfordshire and Luton Archives Service X550-2-6-p128a.

1 Price, *The Flame and the Candle*, p. 144.

2 Hegarty Thorne, *They Put the Flag a-Flyin'*, p. 418.

Anything could be used as an obstacle to block a road. The following four pictures were all taken in North Connacht. They show civilians clearing a tree placed across a road under the watchful eye of some soldiers, a creamery boiler being used to block a road near Manorhamilton (LM) and stone walls being used for a similar purpose near Boyle (RN) (*top right*) and in South Sligo.

Courtesy of Bedfordshire and Luton Archives Service X550-2-6-p96a, X550-2-6_p164a, X550-2-6-p164 (a) and X550-2-6_p118.

Pictured are Michael Kilroy (*standing, left*), Newport (MO), with flying column members Willie Malone and Dr John Madden posing with Lewis and Thompson guns.

The appointment of Mick Kilroy as OC of the West Mayo Brigade, IRA, early in 1921 led to an escalation of the conflict in Mayo. His role in that escalation was recognised by IRA GHQ, who later appointed him to take charge of the 4th Western Division made up of West and North Mayo as well as Connemara. He was described by the British as: 'An ardent Republican. Dangerous, clever and unscrupulous'.[1]

The IRA suffered a major setback at Kilmeena, when British forces killed five IRA men on 19 May 1921. Kilroy's column exacted revenge two weeks later at the Carrowkennedy ambush, 2 June. This was the largest ambush in the west, in terms of fatalities, leaving seven RIC men dead. Despite a major British response the flying column managed to escape.[2]

The IRA was beginning to phase out the use of the large columns by the time of the Truce, as they were difficult to maintain and, while they inflicted large casualties on a couple of occasions, it was felt that smaller units would be more effective.[3]

1 File on Michael Kilroy (TNA: PRO WO 35/207/110).

2 O'Malley, *Raids and Rallies*, pp. 211–71.

3 Augusteijn, *From Public Defiance to Guerrilla Warfare*, p. 137.

As well as ambushes and attacks on the communications network, Republicans sought other ways of frustrating the British war effort. These photographs show a car burned out by the IRA between Ballymote (SO) and Boyle (RN) on 30 June 1921. The car was being employed by the British to transport pigeons which were used in communications. Other examples of this type of activity involved burning huts that were to be used by the Auxiliaries in Tubbercurry (SO) and an oil depot in Sligo town.[1]

Courtesy of Bedfordshire and Luton Archives Service X550-2-6_p111a.

1 Farry, *Sligo: The Irish Revolution 1912–23*, pp. 67–72.

During the early summer of 1921 British forces began to use 'drives' or 'sweeps'. These involved large-scale searches by townland using both the army and the RIC. Pictured (*top*) are people being paraded for identification during a sweep, probably somewhere in Sligo. Also pictured is a joint British Army/RIC search party near Boyle (RN). Very few active Republicans were captured as a result of these efforts and RIC men couldn't be relied upon to identify them. When a sweep was conducted in the Cornamona area of County Galway, one local wrote in a letter intercepted by the British: 'In all the batch they had from Cornamona there were only two IRA soldiers and they had good favour from the police or else they would have gone with the rest'.[1]

Courtesy of Bedfordshire and Luton Archives Service X550-2-6_p128a and X550-2-6 _p96a.

1 Censorship of Mails (TNA: PRO WO 35/180 B).

West Mayo Brigade flying column.

Back row (*left to right*): M. Kilroy, T. Ketterick, E. Moane, J. Gibbons, J. Walsh, P. J. Cannon, P. Lambert, J. Kelly, J. Doherty, B. Malone, J. Rush, J. Ring.

Middle row: M. Naughton, J. Hogan, J. Hearney, D. Sammon, J. Keane, J. Connolly, R. Joyce, P. McNamara, W. Malone.

Front row: D. Gavin, T. Heavy, J. Duffy, J. McDonough, P. Kelly, J. Moran, J. Flaherty, B. Cryan, M. Staunton. Lying in front: Dr J. A. Madden.

By early July the IRA effectively controlled large areas of the west because British forces only came into them occasionally and in large numbers. From midday on 11 July 1921 a Truce came into effect. The last fatality of the War of Independence in this area was in Castlerea (RN), where RIC Sergeant James King was shot dead on the morning of the eleventh. An Irishman, he was alleged to have been involved in attacks on Republicans.[1] This photograph was taken in the days just before the Truce.

1 South Roscommon Brigade Report MS 33,913 (4) (Piaras Béaslaí Papers, National Library of Ireland).

ESTABLISHING A FREE STATE/ DEFENDING THE REPUBLIC

War with the foreigner brings to the fore all that is best and noblest in a nation – civil war all that is mean and base.

IRA leader Frank Aiken, 3 August 1922.[1]

While the military campaign against the British ended with the Truce, the struggle in the prisons continued. This photograph shows suspected Republicans leaving Carrick-on-Shannon (LM) for internment in the Curragh during the War of Independence. During the Truce Jim Brady, an Arigna miner, supervised the building of a tunnel in the Curragh Camp that allowed seventy internees to escape, amongst them a large number of westerners. Two of those involved in the construction of the tunnel were Joe Galvin from Mount Talbot (RN) and Scottie Regan from Keadue (RN). Roscommon escapees included Henry Compton of Kilgefin, Tom Moran of Crossna, Pat Beirne of Clooncunny, Pat McNamara from Culliagh, Strokestown, Jim Farrell from Whitehall and Paddy Barry from Knockvicar, Boyle.[2] The escaped Galway prisoners were Miko and Pat Fleming from Clarenbridge, Michael Roseingrave from Gort, Peter Feeney from Kinvara, John Schley from Clifden and John Manning from Abbey near Ballinasloe.[3]

Courtesy of Bedfordshire and Luton Archives Service X550-2-6-p111a.

1 M. Hopkinson, *Green against Green: The Irish Civil War* (Dublin 2004), p. 273.

2 Hegarty Thorne, *They Put the Flag a-Flyin'*, pp. 116–18.

3 *Connacht Tribune*, 17 December 1921.

Outside the prisons the IRA had come out into the open with recruiting, drilling and reorganisation. Over the next six months they maintained an uneasy relationship with British forces. Newport (MO) man Michael Staines was the liaison officer between Republican and British forces in Galway and Mayo. This was no easy task – resentment simmered underneath the surface and came close to exploding several times, particularly in Galway city where there was a serious altercation at a dance in the Town Hall and a prison riot which saw the jail set on fire. A resumption in hostilities was thought by many to be inevitable.

Courtesy of the Garda Museum.

Eventually a Treaty was agreed which was accepted by 64 to 57 votes in the Dáil. The public were even more strongly pro-Treaty. However, rather than accepting the majority vote, the Dáil and the IRA split into two factions: pro- and anti-Treaty.

The Treaty stipulated that British forces would withdraw from twenty-six of the thirty-two counties; the new Irish Free State would have more power than was available under Home Rule; and there was the potential for regaining at least part of the territory of the newly formed Northern Ireland through the work of the Boundary Commission. However, opponents criticised the ending of the Republic they had sworn to protect and the continued relationship with the Empire. People from both sides worried about the situation in Belfast, where hundreds of nationalists had died with no guarantee that improvement would follow. An inevitable split in the Republican movement followed with Michael Collins and Arthur Griffith the most prominent figures on the pro-Treaty side. Éamon de Valera was the public face of the anti-Treaty side.

Pictured is the wedding photograph of Pádraic Ó Máille, Sinn Féin TD and veteran of the War of Independence from Muintir Eoghain in Connemara (G). Taken in the autumn of 1921 it reflects the nature of the split that occurred in the IRA. The key western IRA men in the photograph went anti-Treaty. The Dublin-based leaders pictured and the Ó Máille family themselves supported the Treaty. Splits of this nature were replicated across the country and some became incredibly bitter with friends and even relations refusing to speak with each other.

Courtesy of Emer Joyce.

Pictured are three active IRA men from South Galway. Pat Coy (*right*) from Derryhoyle, Craughwell (G), 'went' pro-Treaty and was killed in an ambush in Kerry on 27 January 1923. Jack Fahy (*left*) and Dan Ryan (*seated*) both opposed the Treaty, with Ryan being wounded in Clarenbridge in July 1922.

Courtesy of Ryan and Doyle families.

Pictured is Tom Maguire, OC of the IRA's 2nd Western Division (much of South Mayo, East Galway, Roscommon and a tiny portion of Sligo). Maguire, a TD, was instructed by his superior in the IRB to support the Treaty. He was also approached by a number of different priests who urged him to take the pro-Treaty side, with one telling him that the instruction came from the Archbishop of Tuam. While resisting the pressure himself, Maguire felt that church pressure did convince some TDs to support the Treaty.[1]

Courtesy of Mercier Archives.

1 Murray, *Oracles of God*, pp. 42–3.

As well as ideology there were other factors that influenced the decision to oppose or support the Treaty. While there are numerous exceptions, broadly speaking the more active the IRA unit and the more suffering endured at the hands of British forces, the greater the likelihood of its opposing the Treaty. Also the worse the relationship with IRA GHQ, the greater the likelihood of opposition to the Treaty.

Another key factor was the decision of the local IRA leader. Bonds of intense loyalty had developed over the previous years between men who had faced danger together. In West Connemara, IRA Connemara Brigade OC Petie McDonnell opposed the Treaty. The full-time and also the peripheral column men of the West Connemara Brigade (pictured is the flying column of the brigade in 1921) almost uniformly followed his lead. The exceptions were pro-Treaty TD Pádraic Ó Máille, his relations and one other volunteer.

Front row (*left to right*): Brigade OC P. J. McDonnell, C. Breen, R. Joyce, G. Staunton, G. Bartley, J. King, M. Conneely, M. Conroy, J. Feehan.

Back row: J. Mannion, J. Conneely, J. King, P. Bartley, J. Dundass, Patrick Wallace, W. King, P. Keane, W. Conneely, Peter Wallace, T. Madden, J. C. King, D. Keane, T. Coyne.

As a result of the ratification of the Treaty in the Dáil, British forces began to withdraw. All barracks occupied by British forces were handed over to the local IRA unit, whether pro- or anti-Treaty. At the handover of Renmore Barracks (G) are IRA members (*left to right*) Henry Lynch, John Brannigan, John Canavan, Patrick White, Michael Francis, Joseph Kelly, Patrick Feeney and Thomas Kelly (in charge of the guard).

Courtesy of Mellows Barracks.

Pictured is IRA man Lt Seamus O'Brien, in the former RIC barracks in Ballinrobe (MO) after the British withdrawal.

Courtesy of James Dooley.

Both the British Army and the RIC marched out of their barracks to large crowds of well-wishers, friends and those who merely wanted to observe history. Pictured are the Connaught Rangers marching through Eyre Square as they withdraw from Galway city.

Courtesy of Mellows Barracks.

This photograph shows British forces driving out of Athlone.

Courtesy of Athlone Library.

From the spring of 1922 onwards there was an explosion of attacks directed at ex-RIC men: for reasons of revenge, because of their past service, to prevent the occupation of newly purchased farms or to disrupt large landowners who had hired them. On 4 March an RIC man's wife was shot dead during an attack on her husband in Swinford (MO). On 15 March, St Bride's Hospital, above, was entered in Galway city. Two RIC men and an employee of the Congested Districts Board involved in the distribution of land were shot dead, with a third policemen left paralysed. It seems that at least two of the policemen were suspected of involvement in reprisals in Galway during the War of Independence. The policemen were from Mayo, Leitrim and Sligo, and the civilian was from Mayo. April and May also saw ex-RIC men being shot dead in Ballyhaunis (MO) and Newport (MO).[1]

Courtesy of Joe O'Connor.

1 O'Malley and Ó Comhraí, *The Men will Talk to Me*, pp. 49–50; Price, *The Flame and the Candle*, pp. 203–5.

Some RIC men took their chances and remained, others emigrated, sometimes to Northern Ireland where numbers of Catholic RIC men joined the RUC, Northern Ireland's new police force. These included Bill Guilfoyle, brother of Sergeant Michael Guilfoyle (see page 15), pictured here standing on the extreme left.

Courtesy of Michael Guilfoyle.

Others, such as Michael Higgins from Boyle (RN), went further afield. Higgins ended up joining the police in Palestine, by then part of the British Empire.

Courtesy of Martin Higgins.

Despite the support of the churches and the media, Treatyites felt that they were struggling to retain public confidence, partly due to Republican intimidation. IRA units disrupted pro-Treaty rallies, such as in Castlebar (MO) where Michael Collins spoke. They tried to prevent Arthur Griffith speaking in Sligo by prohibiting his meeting. Griffith defied the order and trouble seemed imminent before Billy Pilkington, OC 3rd Western Division, backed down.[1] Pictured is Collins addressing a pro-Treaty rally, probably in Cork.

Courtesy of the National Library of Ireland, Ind_H_0400(1).

There was an urgent need to create a police force and pictured are a number of Mayo recruits to the Civic Guard (An Garda Síochána). Problems in the new force included the anti-Treaty sympathies of a number of the recruits and the resentment many ex-IRA men felt at the employment of ex-RIC men, not all of whom had assisted the Republicans during the War of Independence. The decision to make the force an unarmed one partially developed as a response to a mutiny in their Kildare camp in May 1922.[2]

Courtesy of Michael Ring, TD.

1 M. Farry, *The Aftermath of Revolution: Sligo 1921–23* (Dublin 2000), pp. 59–61.

2 F. McGarry, *Eoin O'Duffy: A Self-Made Hero* (Oxford 2005), pp. 116, 118.

A new National/Free State Army was created to be the army of the pro-Treaty Dáil. It was centred on former IRA men who had taken the pro-Treaty side. Men like Séamus/James Hogan (*left*), often barely out of their teens, were given senior rank, but had little experience of commanding men in battle, training or disciplining them. They were used to being independent of central control and naturally conspiratorial, so there were severe tensions within the army itself, as well as between the army and pro-Treaty civilians, about atrocities carried out by National Army forces and the enforcement of the rule of law. Hogan himself was highly critical of the freedom of action given to the army's regional leadership which led to ill-treatment of prisoners and even murder.[1]

Courtesy of Kilmainham Gaol Museum, 20PO-1A34-08.

1 Hopkinson, *Green against Green*, p. 266.

During the spring of 1922 there were shooting incidents and attacks on barracks as both sides tried to establish their supremacy over different areas. Brigadier George Adamson, whose funeral in Athlone is pictured, was an ex-British soldier who had been involved with the IRA in Westmeath and Roscommon. He joined the National Army and was shot dead in disputed circumstances in Athlone on 25 April 1922. Both pro- and anti-Treaty forces made allegations about each other regarding his death and it was never proven exactly what had happened that night.[1]

Courtesy of Athlone Library.

1 Hegarty Thorne, *They Put the Flag a-Flyin'*, p. 127.

Thousands of loyalists, both Catholic and Protestant, left Ireland or suffered serious harassment and loss during the periods of the Truce and the Civil War. John Talbot Clifton (*pictured*) was a British adventurer with a house in Kylemore in Connemara. When members of the IRA took his car, allegedly with his permission on the assumption that they wouldn't be able to start it, Clifton ambushed them and shot and seriously wounded one of them. Clifton then left the area.[1] In Ballinlough (RN) Henry Benjamin Sampey had his cattle driven and his property and crops destroyed as a result of the support that he gave the crown forces in Castlerea, being a justice of the peace and an army recruiter.[2] William Taylor from Drumshanbo (LM) was persecuted as a suspected informer.[3]

Others, however, sought to take advantage of the situation and the compensation later available to loyalists. In the case of J. P. P. Costello, a recruiter and magistrate from Sligo: 'the real reason for their departure was that they owed very considerable amounts of money ... there had been no persecution'.[4]

Courtesy of Lytham Hall.

1 For details of this case see O'Malley and Ó Comhraí, *The Men Will Talk to Me*, pp. 139–41.

2 Henry Benjamin Sampey (TNA: PRO CO 762/189).

3 William Taylor (TNA: PRO CO 762/23).

4 J. P. P. Costello (TNA: PRO CO 762/7).

Pictured is a girls' orphanage at Clifden (G), one of two run by a Protestant evangelical group, unpopular because of their alleged exploitation of poverty to gain converts. In the summer of 1922 the boys' orphanage was burned by the IRA, who accused the facility of raising orphans for service in the British Army and having provided entertainment for British forces. They also sought specific individuals who they accused of 'espionage'.[1] The master of the orphanage effectively confirmed these charges in a statement made after the burning.[2] The occupants of both orphanages were evacuated to Britain.

Courtesy of the National Library of Ireland, L_Roy_06406.

1 O'Malley and Ó Comhraí, *The Men Will Talk to Me*, pp. 53–5.

2 Colonial Office: Irish Free State Original Correspondence (TNA: PRO CO 739/3).

In the north-east, from 1920 to 1922, thousands fled their homes because of anti-Catholic violence. Pictured are Catholic refugees crowding onto a tram in Belfast. Southern Protestants condemned the violence and in an attempt to defuse the situation publicly refuted charges of southern sectarianism. In Boyle (RN) one group testified in 1920 to: 'the kindness and good-will shown at all times by the Roman Catholics to their Protestant neighbours'.[1]

Belfast, however, began to enter the language of violence in the south, with some Protestants there being told that they had to leave their homes to accommodate refugees arriving from Northern Ireland. The *Church of Ireland Gazette* condemned this development: 'Belfast has nothing to do with the matter. Southern Ireland is the keeper of its own conscience.'[2] The Catholic Church and both pro- and anti-Treaty forces publicly agreed with this sentiment and made efforts to protect Protestants from sectarian or opportunistic attacks. Nevertheless there were attacks and many left. Fearful of a collapse of their community, the *Gazette* began to publish articles expressing the belief that most Catholics didn't support persecution and praising the good behaviour of Republican forces.[3]

Courtesy of Mercier Archives.

1 *The Irish Times*, 22 September 1920.

2 *Church of Ireland Gazette,* 16 June 1922.

3 *Church of Ireland Gazette,* 6, 13 and 27 October 1922.

There was another surge of agrarian agitation in 1922. Lord Ashtown, a large landowner in the area around Woodlawn and Kilconnell, in East Galway, had been at loggerheads with his neighbours for years. Aside from regular land agitation, Ashtown's situation was complicated by his own behaviour: some time previously he dismissed Catholic employees and replaced them with Protestants.[1] In the period between the creation and consolidation of the Free State, his employees and tenants suffered intimidation and attacks.

Courtesy of Irish Military Archives, BMH CD 227/35 (Fintan Murphy Collection).

1 O'Malley and Ó Comhraí, *The Men Will Talk to Me*, pp. 53–4.

To try to halt the slide into physical conflict, pro- and anti-Treaty IRA men held talks and there was even an electoral pact known as the 'panel' between pro- and anti-Treatyite Sinn Féiners in June 1922. This desire for unity frustrated those who wanted to get on with the business of government. Almost inevitably, and at the same time almost unexpectedly, the Civil War began on 28 June 1922. The British government were convinced that the IRA were responsible for the assassination in London of Field Marshal Sir Henry Wilson and insisted that pro-Treaty forces attack IRA headquarters in the Four Courts, Dublin. The final straw for pro-Treatyites came when, in retaliation for the arrest of one of their number, IRA members captured J. J. 'Ginger' O'Connell (*above centre*), previously involved with the IRA in Sligo, and one of the more prominent military men on the pro-Treaty side. Using borrowed British artillery, pro-Treaty forces soon defeated the Republican garrison in the Four Courts, but the violence spread to the rest of the country.

Courtesy of Mercier Archives.

Before the shelling started in Dublin, some rural IRA officers who had been in Dublin returned to their own units. Christie Macken from Inverin (G) returned to Galway, gathered together a number of IRA men and attacked the National Army forces at a coastguard station in Rosaveel (*pictured*) on 2 July, where pro-Treaty forces were garrisoned. After a brief fight the garrison surrendered and were released.[1]

Other IRA officers were less decisive. In the 3rd Western Division there was a debate about what to do. While Frank Carty wanted to attack local pro-Treaty positions, Tom Carney, OC of the East Mayo Brigade, argued in favour of marching on the strategically important town of Athlone. Billy Pilkington argued in favour of marching against British forces in Northern Ireland as a way of reuniting the IRA. Debates of this kind led to paralysis and a failure to take offensive action.[2]

Courtesy of Author's collection.

1 O'Malley and Ó Comhraí, *The Men Will Talk to Me*, p. 139.

2 Farry, *Sligo: The Irish Revolution 1912–23*, p. 98.

Óglaigh na h-Éireann.

DEPARTMENT____________

REFERENCE No.____________

BRIGADE HEADQUARTERS,
EAST CONNEMARA.

Date____________

PROCLAMATION

WHEREAS, it has come to my knowledge that certain persons in this area, known as No. 4 Brigade, 4th. Western Division, are supplying information regarding the movements of our troops to the enemies of the Irish Republic,

AND WHEREAS, certain [illegible] in the aforesaid areaare circulating false reports concerning our Officers and men, and regarding thier conduct in the carrying out of their duties, such statements being detrimental to the Republic,

AND WHEREAS, a similar Proclamation was, some time ago, posted throughout the above area,

NOW I, by virtue of the powers conferred on me as Competent Military Authority of this area of the 4th. Brigade, 4th. Western Division, do hereby give this Notice as a final warning that any person or persons giving such information, or spreading such false reports shall be drastically dealt with.

12/9/22.

Mó Dámhgúnn [illegible]
4. Brigade.

Conscious of the success of the propaganda campaign against British rule in the War of Independence, the pro-Treatyites used the printed word against Republicans. The media, at both local and national level, was almost uniformly pro-Treaty, and Republicans became extremely hostile to it. Terminology such as the word 'irregular', which referred to members of the Republican forces, was developed in order to delegitimise the Republican campaign, and many Republicans found it offensive. Republicans were reduced to information sheets and posters in order to articulate their views and air their grievances. The pictured notice was posted up in Spiddal (G) warning against informing or spreading false information about IRA conduct.

Courtesy of Ó Conláin family.

The arguments advanced by Republicans before the Civil War focused on narrow constitutional issues. The lack of a social agenda frustrated the more radical, who felt the need to broaden the Republican support base. Liam Mellows began to formulate a progressive political programme from Mountjoy Jail, where he had been incarcerated since the fall of the Four Courts. This new programme was published in the media, possibly in a bid to scare conservative elements about the danger of an IRA victory.

Apart from the lack of a social programme, the Republicans' most senior political leader, Éamon de Valera (*centre*), was sidelined almost as soon as the first shots were fired. His status as president of the Republic was not exploited as effectively as it might have been. On the right of the picture above is P. J. Ruttledge, Republican TD for Mayo North and West. When de Valera was arrested Ruttledge became acting president of the Republic.[1]

Courtesy of Kilmainham Gaol Museum, 21PC-1K42-20.

1 C. O'Malley and A. Dolan, *No Surrender Here!: The Civil War Papers of Ernie O'Malley 1922–1924* (Dublin 2007), p. 572.

Outside Dublin, Republicans burned their barracks and took to the hills, sniping and ambushing incursions into their territory by pro-Treaty forces, but rarely leaving it and usually only then in raids designed to capture materials and supplies rather than for any strategic benefit. Pictured is Renmore Barracks, Galway, abandoned and burned by the Republicans in July 1922.

Courtesy of Mellows Barracks.

Republican forces also destroyed communications, which caused unemployment, food shortages and even death because of damaged bridges and roads. The inconvenience and danger was bitterly resented by the local population. Pictured are a damaged bridge in Leitrim and the Marconi Wireless Station near Clifden (G) burned by IRA forces in the summer of 1922. Not all Republicans were so tactless. From West Mayo it was reported that Republicans were sharing captured provisions with their civilian supporters, 'thus keeping a certain class on their side'.[1]

Bridge courtesy of Getty Images; Marconi Station courtesy of the National Library of Ireland, L_Cab 04374.

1 Report 6 April 1923 in General Weekly Reports for Claremorris Command (CW/OPS/03/6, Military Archives).

The war was originally fought in a good spirit. Pictured are captured National Army soldiers, who are also photographed playing football in Campbell's field in Swinford (MO) while being guarded by the IRA. Also pictured is a wounded soldier whose wounds were tended by Tom Murray, Medical Officer, East Mayo Brigade IRA.

Three images courtesy of Pádhraig Campbell.

Loyalty was fluid, and both sides struggled to ensure that personal loyalty wouldn't prove stronger than political loyalty. Patrick Joseph Geary, from the Claddagh in Galway city, opposed the Treaty, but when he was arrested he was smuggled out of prison by a friend on the opposing side.

Courtesy of Ciarán Lenoach.

As the new National Army forces marched into barracks all over the west, they were often greeted as liberators, since Republican forces had alienated some in the community because of the commandeering of food, cars, etc., and what was seen as the bullying of former or current political opponents. Efforts were made by the National Army to send soldiers to their home areas, when possible, particularly former IRA men who were perceived as having been effective against British forces during the War of Independence.

Pictured is the Ballygar garrison on the Galway/Roscommon border. Enthusiasm waned at their arrival when they did not quickly defeat the Republicans and their behaviour was less than ideal. The failure of the army to keep them adequately supplied led to the running up of massive, sometimes unpaid, bills.

In Tuam (G) one pro-Treaty TD complained about the army, commenting that the local population was 'almost anxious' to have the Republicans return.[1]

In Sligo Unionist landowner Captain Gray Wynne thought even more favourably of the Republicans, saying they had 'the courage of their convictions' and 'appeared better disciplined than the Free State Army'.[2]

Courtesy of Roscommon County Library.

1 Price, *The Flame and the Candle*, p. 238.

2 M. Bence-Jones, *Twilight of the Ascendancy* (London 1987), p. 229.

The Arigna Mining Company had a similarly negative opinion of the National Army. During the War of Independence the company had supplied coal to British forces, and they were threatened and the IRA raided the homes of the directors. Afterwards the mines were seized by Republican forces and almost 2,000 tonnes of coal sold by them. However, when National Army forces drove the IRA from the mine: 'It was alleged that the Free State Troops did very considerable material damage unnecessarily and raided and looted the company's residence'.[1]

Courtesy of the Arigna Mining Experience.

1 Arigna Mining Company (TNA: PRO CO 762/19).

The National Army ran the war in the west primarily from Limerick and Athlone. Seán Mac Eoin of Longford (*pictured*) was OC of the Athlone Command. Mac Eoin had a reputation as a brave and chivalrous War of Independence leader. During the Civil War he treated well the OC of the IRA's 2nd Western Division, Tom Maguire, when he was captured, and he was also credited with interceding on behalf of Michael Kilroy to protect him from execution. Despite that, Republican folklore in the west could be negative towards him because of the January 1923 executions of Republican prisoners in Athlone and his failure or disinclination to maintain military discipline. Significantly more unpopular was his second in command, Tony Lawlor, a man who clearly prided himself on his toughness. Lawlor was almost as hard on his own troops as he was on his enemies. He once shot a prisoner, Patrick Mulrennan (of Kiltymaine, Liscaul, close to the Roscommon/Mayo border), dead in Athlone during a prison riot, then boasted about it in a letter to his mother: 'It was a wonderful shot.'[1] Mulrennan's brother Seamus was shot dead during an attack on pro-Treaty forces shortly afterwards at Liscaul.[2]

Courtesy of Mercier Archives.

1 Tom Maguire interview (P17b/100, O'Malley notebooks, UCD Archives); Hopkinson, *Green against Green*, p. 216.

2 Price, *The Flame and the Candle*, pp. 253, 259.

Pictured are men queuing to join the National Army in Athlone. One of the major problems faced at the outset of the Civil War by the pro-Treaty side was lack of numbers, which could only be solved by rapid expansion. By the end of the war the army contained a large number of ex-British soldiers, which antagonised Republicans but from the pro-Treaty perspective gave its army the advantage of experienced soldiers with no ties of loyalty to previous comrades.

Courtesy of Athlone Library.

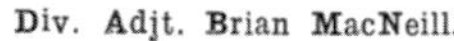

Div. Adjt. Brian MacNeill.

Brigadier Seamus Devins.

Capt. Harry Benson.

Lieut. Paddy Carroll.

Vol. Joseph Banks.

Vol. Thos. Langan.

The war soon became bitter. Sligo provided some of the most serious resistance to the Free State of any county. During sweeps of the area around Benbulben (SO), members of the National Army killed six members of the IRA, pictured above. Despite an attempt to cover up the deaths of 'Sligo's Noble Six', it quickly became clear that foul play was involved. According to a soldier who was present, their killers were 'the two captains and four of the former British soldiers.'[1] While Republicans tended to highlight the role of ex-soldiers in atrocities, some of the worst offenders had been active IRA men during the War of Independence.

Courtesy of Irish Military Archives CD 250/5/15.

1 Hopkinson, *Green against Green*, p. 215.

Despite the loss of large numbers of men and weapons, Republicans were still capable of mounting major operations. Furious at the capture of Ballina (MO) by Republicans led by Mick Kilroy in September 1922, the National Army mounted a major campaign against the IRA in Mayo and Western Sligo. During that campaign Joe Ring, the most senior War of Independence veteran in Mayo to support the Treaty, was killed. Here he is pictured standing in front of 'The Big Fella' armoured car with one leg crossed in front of the other, along with other members of the National Army.[1]

Courtesy of Michael Ring TD.

1 Price, *The Flame and the Candle*, pp. 227–8.

The pro-Treaty side was given very prominent public support by the Catholic hierarchy, who excommunicated Republicans who continued to resist the Free State in October 1922. Few clergymen publicly endorsed the anti-Treaty side, although privately significant numbers had anti-Treaty sympathies, particularly in the west. Other priests, who had been their bitter opponents during the War of Independence, now enthusiastically promoted pro-Treaty ex-IRA men. Monsignor Patrick McAlpine, parish priest of Clifden (*above*), had been a 'bitter opponent of Sinn Féin'[1] but became an enthusiastic supporter of Pádraic Ó Máille, TD, describing him as: 'a sterling Irishman, a practising Catholic and a wise statesman'.[2]

Courtesy of Mercy Archives, Galway.

1 Alice Cashel, BMH WS 366, p. 7.

2 *Connacht Tribune*, 18 August 1923.

Another large-scale operation by Republicans was the capture on 29 October 1922 of the town of Clifden (G). Led by the newly appointed OC of the 4th Western Division, Petie McDonnell (West Connemara Brigade), Volunteers were used from all over the divisional area. In fighting that lasted all day, one National Army soldier, Thomas Conneely from Clynagh near Carraroe (G), was killed. Two Republicans from Knockmore (MO), Pat Morrison and Thomas James, were shot, having surrendered to National Army forces. Despite the capture of a hundred rifles, this Republican success was not built upon and, after extensive sweeps, Connemara was largely pacified by the end of the year.[1] Pictured are Pat Morrison (*right*) and a commemoration in Mayo for Morrison and James shortly after the end of the Civil War.

Images courtesy of John William Morrison.

1 O'Malley and Ó Comhraí, *The Men Will Talk to Me*, pp. 168, 279.

In retaliation for the government executing Republicans, Pádraic Ó Máille TD (*pictured*) was shot and wounded and another TD, Seán Hales, was shot dead in Dublin on 7 December. As a reprisal the government executed four Mountjoy prisoners who were uninvolved in the assassination, none of whom had been tried. Amongst them was Liam Mellows. While the executions had no legal basis, they were effective and the policy of targeting TDs was shelved. Ó Máille was horrified at the executions and was aware of the need for reconciliation in the aftermath of the Civil War. Early the following year, despite his wounds not being fully healed, he told a public meeting in Tuam: 'Tá mé sásta lámh an té a chuir na piléir ionam a chroitheadh.' (I'm happy to shake the hand of the person who put the bullets in me.)[1]

Courtesy of Emer Joyce.

1 Bairéad, *Gan Baisteadh*, p. 114.

For many, the policy of executing prisoners reduced the legitimacy of the state and its government, even amongst those who weren't active anti-Treatyites. Pictured is Patrick Beattie, who had been captain of the Rahara (RN) Company of the IRA during the War of Independence and had stayed neutral in the Civil War. He knew and respected Rory O'Connor, one of the four executed in reprisal for the shooting of Hales and Ó Máille, and the execution alienated him from the leadership of the Free State.[1]

Courtesy of Frank Beattie.

1 Information from his son Frank.

Aside from the executions, the other behaviour most closely associated with the Civil War was the destruction of the big houses of the landed class. These burnings actually began during the War of Independence and had a number of motivations. Outside of Cork, burnings in vengeance for British reprisals seem to have been rare, although Protestants had been threatened with revenge attacks in Leitrim in the event of further British reprisals.[1] A feature of the conflict in Roscommon was the burning of houses of suspected informers.[2] IRA units also burned big houses to prevent them being used as barracks by either British or National Army forces. It was for this reason that Castlehackett House (G) (*above*) was burned on 11 January 1923. Before burning the house, the IRA told its occupant, Colonel Bernard, that it was being done as a military necessity and that he was well regarded by the people of the area.[3]

Courtesy of the Irish Architectural Archive, 022_024X_002.

1 Charles Pinkman, BMH WS 1263, p. 9.

2 Report of the First Battalion South Roscommon Brigade February 1921 (P7A/38, Mulcahy Papers, UCD Archives).

3 N. Ó Gadhra, *Civil War in Connacht 1922–1923* (Cork 1999), pp. 64–5.

Castlegrove House (G) was another of the properties burned during the Civil War, on 25 July 1922. However, in this case the IRA issued a statement denying their involvement and it was believed locally that agrarian agitators took advantage of the general upheaval of the period to burn the house.[1]

Courtesy of the Irish Architectural Archive, 030_056_X_001.

1 Ó Gadhra, *Civil War in Connacht 1922–1923*, p. 33.

Active support for the Free State was another reason for the targeting of some houses, and this was probably why Moore Hall (MO) was burned on 1 February 1923. Maurice Moore was a Free State senator. The fact that relations of pro-Treaty supporters were being targeted, and also the similarity with burnings carried out by British forces as reprisals during the War of Independence, proved counter-productive for the Republicans. A complicating factor in the case of Moore Hall was land that was the subject of a long-running agrarian agitation. During the Civil War the belief arose that, as the land was being divided, supporters of the pro-Treaty position were being given preference over anti-Treatyites.[1]

Courtesy of Irish Architectural Archive, 011_064_X_007.

1 Price, *The Flame and the Candle*, pp. 247–8.

By 1923 thousands of IRA men were imprisoned, with the attendant strain on families and incomes. Pictured (*right*) is a postcard sent to a Gort (G) prisoner during his Civil War imprisonment. The inability of active Republicans to live in any kind of comfort also corroded morale. In October 1922 National Army intelligence reported from Westport (MO) that the Republicans: 'seem to be in a very bad way, clothes are torn and ragged, boots broken and their appearance unkempt. They seem to be properly fed up.'[1]

A number of leading IRA officers started publicly to call for an end to the fighting. Among them was Thomas 'Baby' Duggan (*c.* 1899–1925, *pictured above*) from Roscam, close to Oranmore (G).[2] Nicknamed Baby because of his strong physique, he was involved in the Easter Rising in 1916. Interned in Frongoch, he was active in the War of Independence, taking part in the Merlin Park and Kilroe ambushes, and became the quartermaster of the Mid-Galway Brigade, IRA. British forces burnt his family home. Wounded three times in the Civil War he was eventually captured by National Army forces in October 1922.[3]

Postcard courtesy of Private Collection; Image of Duggan courtesy of John Commins.

1 Intelligence Report, 7 October 1922 (CW/OPS/02/01/02, Military Archives).

2 *Connacht Tribune,* 10 February 1923.

3 *Ibid.,* 22 October 1922.

As the Republic declared in 1916 and ratified, as Republicans saw it, by the electorate in 1918 as well as the Dáil, collapsed around them, the Republicans' most negative characteristics became distilled into a poison. Allegations, not always made by those hostile to Republicans, of robbery and murder were levelled at various Republican leaders. In November 1922 Frank Carty had two men executed as informers near Tubbercurry (SO), a decision that caused Republican as well as pro-Treaty criticism.[1] Carty attracted much negative comment and allegations of murder and robbery from pro-Treatyites, which were bitterly contested by Carty and his supporters.[2] Despite the hostility, which lasted beyond the end of the Civil War, he was elected to the Dáil in 1923 and at every subsequent election. He served as a Fianna Fáil TD for fifteen years, until his death in 1942. This photograph was taken in the 1930s.

Courtesy of NUI Galway.

1 Farry, *The Aftermath of Revolution*, p. 87.

2 Murray, *Oracles of God*, pp. 75, 118.

The funeral of Thomas Hughes from Bogganfin, Roscommon, passing through Athlone, 1924. Hughes, an IRA man, was executed on 20 January 1923 for being caught in armed opposition to the Free State, along with four Galway men – Mick Walsh (Caherlistrane), Martin Burke (Caherlistrane), Hubert Collins (Keekill, Headford) and Stephen Joyce (Caherlistrane) – in Athlone military barracks. There was a clear move by the Free State government to provincialise the executions as a way of maximising impact. It was said that Hughes' mother, who lived close to Athlone, heard the shots that killed her son.[1]

Courtesy of Athlone Library.

1 Information from Frank Beattie.

Pictured seated on the extreme right of this photograph is Agnes Walsh (née Cotter). It was taken at a family wedding in the 1950s. It is hard to imagine that the elderly woman in the photograph played a major role in the escape of fourteen Republican prisoners from Galway Jail in March 1923, organising contact between the IRA and a sympathetic soldier. Seven of the prisoners were from Galway, six from Mayo and one from Tipperary. Originally from Rosaveel (G), she was widowed by members of the British forces who took her husband from their shop and public house in Galway city and shot him dead in October 1920. By the end of the Civil War the business was almost choked out of existence by the financial support she was giving Republicans.[1]

Courtesy of Garry Walsh.

1 O'Malley and Ó Comhraí, *The Men Will Talk to Me*, pp. 203–7.

April 1923 saw one last major attack in the west when Christie Macken and Vincent Corcoran led an assault on Headford Barracks (G). At least two National Army soldiers were killed, with one Republican being shot dead and another being seriously wounded and dying young some years later. Six Republicans, five from Galway – Frank (Proinsias) Cunnane (Kilcoona, Headford), Séamus Ó Máille (Oughterard), Seán Newell (Headford), Martin Moylan (Annaghdown) and Michael Monaghan (Clooneen, Headford) – and the younger brother of Tom Maguire, Seán (Cross, Mayo), were taken from Galway Jail, transported to Tuam Workhouse and executed. Those men and the five executed in Athlone in January came to be known as the Eleven Galway Martyrs.

Courtesy of Mercier Archives.

Liam Lynch (*pictured*), chief of staff of the IRA for most of the Civil War, seems to have lost all sense of reality regarding the position the IRA was in towards the end of the war, refusing to consider ending the conflict. He was eventually run to ground in the Knockmealdown mountains and mortally wounded, dying in Clonmel. He was replaced as chief of staff by Frank Aiken, who had been reluctant to involve himself in the war and was more realistic about the nature of the conflict. Orders were issued to cease hostilities and then to dump arms in May 1923.

Courtesy of Mercier Archives.

Despite the official end of the hostilities, violence motivated by political and agrarian concerns continued. In Mayo for example John Melvin was beaten, shot dead and labelled as an informer close to Swinford. John McGeehin, a pro-Treatyite ex-member of Belmullet District Council, died after his house was fired into.[1]

A number of the Civic Guard were viciously attacked by Republicans. James Mulroy (*pictured*) a Straide (MO) man, was given the Scott medal for bravery for confronting armed men in Clare – he was wounded in the process. Guards were also in danger from regular criminals and even members of the National Army. Investigations revealed that in the second half of 1923, current or demobilised soldiers were guilty or suspected of 60% of murders and 50% of sexual offences, for example.[2]

Courtesy of Garda Museum.

1 Price, *The Flame and the Candle*, p. 256.

2 Murray, *Oracles of God*, p. 75.

Eventually only the most senior, the most active and the most violent of the anti-Treaty IRA remained imprisoned. Some had been sentenced to prison terms, most hadn't. Jack Keogh of Ballinasloe (G), who drew the pictured cartoon which reads: 'The last of the Irregulars to leave Tintown 19–?', was sentenced to ten years imprisonment for a litany of offences after the end of the Civil War, primarily directed at the Civic Guard and at those who were felt to have assisted the British state. In 1926 he escaped and emigrated to Chicago before eventually returning to live in Ballinasloe.[1] Note that, under the figure, the cartoon also says: 'I am not conquered yet.'

Courtesy of Tim Buckley.

1 Ó Comhraí, *Gaillimh 1913–23*.

Within the internment camps, Republicans attempted to maintain their discipline and structure. This photograph of the Hare Park (Curragh) Camp Council was taken after the end of the Civil War with a camera smuggled into the camp inside a chicken. Amongst those pictured is Tom Derrig (1897–1956) (*front left*), OC of the West Mayo Brigade at the time of his arrest by British forces in January 1921 and adjutant-general of the anti-Treaty headquarters when he was re-arrested in April 1923. Sitting beside him is Paul Bofin of Rosses Point (SO). Active in the Arigna (RN) area, he had previously escaped from Sligo Jail. Second from the left, back row, is Jack Comer of Galway.[1]

Courtesy of Mercier Archives.

1 Hegarty Thorne, *They Put the Flag a-Flyin'*, p. 216.

For many Republicans the future looked bleak. One of those executed on 20 January 1923 in Athlone was Martin Burke from Caherlistrane (G) who wanted to be remembered as the 'wild boy of the family'. His brother Jim (*pictured*) received the following letter from him:

> To dear Jim,
>
> Just a few lines before I pass away from this world forever. I suppose my time has come. So don't cry for my sake. Life is sweet but we are getting a good chance at preparing for tomorrow. Poor Tom Hughes is by my side, a soldier to the last. Stephen Joyce, Mick Walsh and Hubert Collins are going before God in the morning. I think with God's help I'm prepared to die. I don't know where this will find you but I will direct it to Ballinapark, the spot I loved best. Poor old Dad. This will give him a blow, but it's a chance for a happy death. So Goodbye until we meet in the happy land beyond the skies.
>
> Goodbye from your Loving Brother,
>
> Martin J. Burke.

Leaving prison disillusioned, unable to find regular employment in a country where the vast majority of employers were supporters of the Treatyite position, Jim left for America.[1] Thousands of anti-Treatyites left with him and many of them never returned.

Courtesy of Eileen Collins.

1 Information from Gabriel Burke and Eileen Collins.

CONCLUSION

People dealt with the agony of defeat in different ways. Some became bitter, some threw themselves into the GAA, the language movement, greyhound racing, writing or religion. Others went into politics. Nobody was quite sure what would come next and then, a boost. Despite their most committed supporters still being under lock and key, the anti-Treatyites gained one vote in four in the 1923 general election. Within a short space of time the vast majority of anti-Treaty Republicans began to support Éamon de Valera's new Fianna Fáil party which entered the Dáil.

By 1932 Fianna Fáil was the governing party. To some degree the early years of Fianna Fáil reflected the revolution: there was a desire to prove themselves, to reform, to experiment, to accommodate all sections of society within the same movement and, like the revolution, this saw both success and failure.

The idea of national unity remained important to a large cross-section of the population of the southern state. There was residual sympathy for men on the run or those who died for 'the cause', even after de Valera's government executed members of the IRA in the 1940s.

Unsurprisingly, as time passed the Republican veterans lived hugely different lives. Some remained radical, some became cornerstones of the establishment. Some of those who received recognition deserved it, some didn't. As time went on the community forgot and simplified events as all communities do. The Civil War was only mentioned by the impolite or to mobilise voters. Republicans made a point of honouring their dead publicly; there have also been a number of monuments raised to those who died in the service of the British during the First World War, but places where National Army soldiers fell in action during the Civil War remain unmarked.

The more awkward aspects of the period dropped out of the public consciousness. The use of violence by members of the IRA to enforce the boycott of the police and the violence directed at ex-policemen and loyalists during the Truce, as well as the lack of guerrilla activity in most parts of the country, were filtered out. Also forgotten was the enthusiasm with which the First World War was greeted, how a large number of people attempted to take advantage of events, the support British forces received from a large section of the population, even while engaging in reprisals, and the role of Irishmen in RIC reprisals.

One reason for the amnesia was the fact that many former revolutionaries spoke little to their families about events they had been involved in. The son of one veteran I interviewed described being caught, as a child, smiling when his father was

Pictured at the grave of Thomas James, killed at Clifden (G) on 29 October 1922, wearing the cap, is John Bourke of Knockmore (MO). He spoke little to his family of his involvement in the IRA during the course of which he escaped from the Curragh, was on hunger strike and came close to being executed. Like most of his contemporaries he went on to live a normal, uneventful life.

Courtesy of Anthony Bourke.

trying to manage an IRA veteran who was clearly struggling to deal psychologically with the events he had been involved in: 'Some day I'll tell you a story and then you won't laugh at Bill.'

This book is my effort at telling Bill's story, regardless of what side he fought for.

BIBLIOGRAPHY

Unpublished Sources

Military Archives, Dublin

Bureau of Military History Papers (BMH Witness Statements also consulted in National Archives, Dublin)

Civil War Operations Reports

National Library, Dublin

Maj.-General Patrick O'Daly Statement P4548

P. Ó hEidhin, 'I Remember Mellows', MS 15,289

Piaras Béaslaí papers

University College Dublin Archives

Fitzgerald Papers

Mulcahy Papers

O'Malley Papers

Twomey Papers

National University of Ireland, Galway

F.S. Chevers, Chevers of Killyan (NUI Galway LE (20))

Pol 4 'Papers Relating to the deaths of Patrick and Harry Loughnane'

P. J. McDonnell, 'West Connemara IRA Organisation and Operation'

National Archives, Dublin

Department of Justice Files, Mountjoy Jail

National Archives, Kew, London

Various papers relating to the Colonial Office (CO), Home Office (HO), War Office (WO), Irish Grants Committee (CO 762)

Newspapers

An t-Óglách

Church of Ireland Gazette

Connacht Tribune

East Galway Democrat

Freeman's Journal, The

Galway Express, The

Irish Bulletin

Irish Independent

Irish Times, The

Leitrim Observer

Roscommon Herald

Tuam Herald

Anecdotal Information

Anthony Bourke, Tim Buckley, Gabriel Burke, Eileen Collins, John Corry, Daniel and Therese Corry, James Dooley, Seán and Eileen Glynn, David Grant, Pat Margetts, Kathleen Mannion, John William Morrison, Gerry and William O'Hanlon, Emer Joyce, Seán Ó Súilleabháin, John and Éamonn Reilly, Paddy and Mary Ryan, Joe and Nancy Stanford, Frank Beattie, Paul Blake, Paul Browne, Padhraig Campbell, John Commins, Michael Farry, Enda Folan, John Francis Gannon, Seán Gannon, Patsy Graham, Michael Guilfoyle, Dónal 'Mox' Henderson, Martin Higgins, Dr Tim Horgan, Carmel Hughes, Pádraig Keane, Ciarán Lenoach, Cóilín Mac Donncha, Kevan Murphy, Honor Ó Brolchain, Mártan Ó Ciardha, Seosamh Ó Cuaig, Finian Ó Fathaigh, Maitiú Ó Flatharta, Seán Ó Flatharta, Peadar Ó Máille, Cormac O'Malley, Seán Ó Neachtain, Rory O'Shaughnessy, Sandy Perceval, Eunan Sweeney, Tom Toomey, Kathleen Villiers-Tuthill, Anne Walsh, Garry Walsh, Theresa Walsh, Irene Whelan, Michael Whelan, and Emma Williams.

Internet Sources

www.cairogang.com

www.census.nationalarchives.ie

www.irishnewsarchives.com
www.warofindependence.info

Published Sources

Abbott, R., *Police Casualties in Ireland, 1919–1922* (Cork, 2000)
Augusteijn, J., *From Public Defiance to Guerrilla Warfare: The Experience of Ordinary Volunteers in the Irish War of Independence* (Dublin, 1996)
Bairéad, T., *Gan Baisteadh* (Baile Átha Cliath, 1972)
Bence-Jones, M., *Twilight of the Ascendancy* (London, 1987)
'Body of "informer" shot in 1920 to be reburied', *Connacht Tribune*, 10 July 1998
Breathnach, C., *The Congested Districts Board of Ireland, 1891–1923* (Dublin, 2005)
Campbell, F., *Land and Revolution: Nationalist Politics in the West of Ireland 1891–1921* (Oxford, 2005)
Cole, J. A., *Lord Haw-Haw* (London, 1964)
Deasy, L., 'The Schull Peninsula in the War of Independence', in *Éire-Ireland* (Summer 1966), pp. 5–18
Dolan, M., 'Galway 1920–1921' in *Capuchin Annual* 1970, pp. 384–95
Evidence on Conditions in Ireland (Washington, 1921)
Farry, M., *Sligo 1914–1921: A Chronicle of Conflict* (Trim, 1992)
— *The Aftermath of Revolution: Sligo, 1921–23* (Dublin, 2000)
— *Sligo: The Irish Revolution 1912–23* (Dublin, 2012)
Foy, M. T., *Michael Collins's Intelligence War* (Gloucestershire, 2006)
Gaughan, J. A., *The Memoirs of Constable Jeremiah Mee* (Cork, 2012)
Greaves, C. D., *Liam Mellows and the Irish Revolution* (Belfast, 2004)
Hart, P., *The I.R.A. and its Enemies* (Oxford, 1998)
— *The I.R.A. at War 1916–1923* (Oxford, 2005)
Hegarty Thorne, K., *They Put the Flag a-Flyin': The Roscommon Volunteers 1916–1923* (Oregon, 2007)
Henry, W., *Galway and the Great War* (Cork, 2006)
— *Forgotten Heroes: Galway Soldiers of the Great War 1914–1918* (Cork, 2007)
— *Blood for Blood: The Black and Tan War in Galway* (Cork, 2012)
Hogan, D. (Frank Gallagher), *The Four Glorious Years* (Dublin, 1953)

Hopkinson, M., *The Irish War of Independence* (Dublin, 2002)

— *Green against Green: The Irish Civil War* (Dublin, 2004 edition)

IRA Jailbreaks 1918–1921 (Cork, 2010)

Kenneally, I., *The Paper Wall: Newspapers and Propaganda in Ireland 1919–1921* (Cork, 2008)

Kenny, T., *Galway: Politics and Society, 1910–23* (Dublin, 2011)

Leeson, D., *The Black and Tans: British Police and Auxiliaries in the Irish War of Independence* (Oxford, 2011)

Matthews, A., *Renegades: Irish Republican Women 1900–1922* (Cork, 2010)

McGarry, F., *Eoin O'Duffy: A Self-Made Hero* (Oxford, 2005)

Mac Giolla Choille, B., *Intelligence Notes, 1913–1916* (Dublin, 1966)

McMahon, T., *Pádraig Ó Fathaigh's War of Independence: Recollections of a Galway Gaelic Leaguer* (Cork, 2000)

McNamara, C., *Revolution in the West of Ireland 1913–21* (Dublin, 2014)

Mitchell, A., *Revolutionary Government in Ireland: Dáil Éireann 1919–22* (Dublin, 1995)

Mitchell, A. and Ó Snodaigh, P., *Irish Political Documents 1916–1949* (Dublin, 1985)

Moffitt, M., *Soupers and Jumpers: The Protestant Missions in Connemara 1838–1937* (Dublin, 2008)

Moran, M., *Executed for Ireland: The Patrick Moran Story* (Cork, 2010)

Murray, P., *Oracles of God: The Roman Catholic Church and Irish Politics 1922–37* (Dublin, 2000)

Ó Comhraí, C., *Gaillimh 1913–23* (Gailimh, 2013)

Ó Gadhra, N., *Civil War in Connacht 1922–1923* (Cork, 1999)

Ó Laoi, P., *Fr. Griffin 1892–1920* (Galway, 1994)

— *History of Castlegar Parish* (Galway, 1996)

O'Mahony, S., *Frongoch: University of Revolution* (Dublin, 1987)

O'Malley, C. (ed.), *Rising Out: Seán Connolly of Longford* (Dublin, 2007)

O'Malley, C. and Dolan, A., *No Surrender Here! The Civil War Papers of Ernie O'Malley, 1922–1924* (Dublin, 2007)

O'Malley, C. and Ó Comhraí, C., *The Men Will Talk to Me: Galway Interviews by Ernie O'Malley* (Cork, 2013)

O'Malley, Ernie, *On Another Man's Wound* (Cork, 2013)

— *Raids and Rallies* (Cork, 2011)

Ó Ruairc, P. Óg, *Revolution: A Photographic History of Revolutionary Ireland* (Cork, 2011)

Pinkman, J. A., *In the Legion of the Vanguard* (Cork, 1998)

Plunkett Dillon, G., *All in the Blood* (Dublin, 2006)

Price, D., *The Flame and the Candle: War in Mayo 1919–1924* (Cork, 2012)

Regan, J. M., *The Irish Counter-Revolution 1921–1936* (Dublin, 1999)

Toomey, T., *The War of Independence in Limerick 1912–1921* (Limerick, 2010)

Townshend, C., *The British Campaign in Ireland, 1919–1921* (Oxford, 1975)

With the IRA in the Fight for Freedom: 1919 to the Truce (Cork, 2010)

ACKNOWLEDGEMENTS

To the staff of the various archives and facilities who have made their resources and expertise available to me over the years. Míle buíochas mar sin le: Niall Bergin and Anne-Marie Ryan and the staff of Kilmainham Gaol Museum; Nigel Lutt and B. A. Marvin of the Bedfordshire and Luton Archives Service; Anthony Leonard (grandson of Jack Leonard who took some iconic shots of the period in the west), P. J. Maloney of Mellows Barracks, Galway; Kieran Hoare and the staff of the James Hardiman Library, National University of Ireland, Galway; Gearóid O'Brien (head librarian) and the staff of Athlone Library; Derryglad Folk Museum, County Roscommon; Caitlín Browne and Roscommon County Library; Clare County Library; Galway City Museum; all the staff of Military Archives, Cathal Brugha Barracks, Dublin; the director and staff of the National Archives, Dublin; the National Archives, Kew, London; Martin Drew and the Garda Museum; Getty Images; The Imperial War Museum, London; Lytham Hall Archive; Mike Galer and the 9th and 12th Royal Lancers Museum; The Queen's Royal Lancers Museum; Link4life, Local Studies, Rochdale; www.irishnewsarchives.com (a treasure trove of old newspapers, both national and local, and worth spending time on); the staff of The National Library, Dublin; The Police Museum, Belfast; Colum O'Riordan of the Irish Architectural Archive; Colm Keane of The Arigna Mining Experience; David Grant of www.cairogang.com (an incredible website compiled by a man who is passionate about his history and equally passionate about sharing it); Brian Crowley of the Pearse Museum, Dublin; John Cunningham of The Irish Labour History Society; David Hume of The Grand Orange Lodge of Ireland; The Argyll and Sutherland Highlanders Museum;

Kennys Bookshop, Galway; The Irish Jesuit Archive; An Gúm; Seamus Helferty and UCD Archives; Tomás Mac Conmara of Cuimhneamh an Chláir; Cashel Folk Museum; Pat Burdick and Colby College, Maine, who are the curators of the James Brendan Connolly collection; Kieran Waldron and Tuam Diocesan Archives; Mercy Archives, Galway; and University College Cork.

For information, photographs and hospitality, many thanks to the Bourke, Breathnach, Burke, Collins, Corry (Ballyhooley), Corry (Loughrea), Doyle, Foley, Glynn, Goode, James, Margetts, Morrison, Ó Conláin, Ó Flatharta, O'Hanlon, O'Malley, Ó Súilleabháin, Reilly, Ryan, Stanford and Walsh families, and for all the help and assistance given during the course of this research. Many thanks for the same reason to Ashling and Anthony Bourke, Pamela Aldrich, Frank Beattie, Deirdre Breathnach, David Bockett, Paul Blake, Paul Browne, Tim Buckley, Padhraig Campbell, John Commins, Cllr Dermot Connolly, Dominic Cronin, Cumann Béaloideasa Chonamara, Cumann Seanchais Chois Fharraige, Pádraig de Bhaldraithe, Aoife de Blácam, James Dooley, Mary Dwyer, Michael Farry, John Flaherty, Enda Folan, Gavin Foster, John Francis Gannon, Seán Gannon, John Garvey, J. Anthony Gaughan, Patsy Graham, Michael Guilfoyle, Mary Harris, An Cásach Gary Hastings, Paddy Hayes, Brendan Healy, Dónal 'Mox' Henderson, Séamus Hickey, Jim Higgins, Martin Higgins, Bernie Hughes, Brian Hughes, Dr Tim Horgan, Carmel Hughes, Emer Joyce, Pádraig Keane, Barry Kelly, Vincent Kelly, Seán Kyne TD, Mícheál Lally, Ciarán Lenoach, Proinsias Mac an Bheatha, Barra Mac Aodha Bhuí (An Gúm), Seosamh Mac Donnchadha, Joe McBride, Betty McGowan, Timothy McMahon, Niall Meehan, Kevan Murphy, Mait Ó Brádaigh, Honor Ó Brolchain, Eoin Ó Carra, Mícheál Ó Catháin, Aindrias Ó Cathasaigh, Mártan Ó Ciardha, Mícheál Ó Conaire, Breandán Ó Conláin, Bernie O'Connell, Joe O'Connor of joeoconnorphotography.com, Louise O'Connor, Seosamh Ó Cuaig, Peadar O'Dowd, Finian Ó Fathaigh, Peadar Ó Máille, Cormac O'Malley, An t-Ath. Fiontán Ó Monacháin, Seán Ó Neachtain, Rory O'Shaughnessy, Sandy Perceval, Dominic Price, Bob Quinn, Diana Quinn, Tomás Quinn, Michael Ring TD, Fr Liam Ryan, Averil Staunton of

Historical Ballinrobe, Eunan Sweeney, Kathy Hegarty Thorne and Lew Thorne, Tom Toomey, Kathleen Villiers-Tuthill, Anne Walsh, Garry Walsh, Theresa Walsh, Irene Whelan, Michael Whelan and Emma Williams.

A thousand thanks to the staff of Mercier Press who managed to make a book out of what I gave them, and for giving me the opportunity to publish it. Thank you Mary, Sarah, Wendy, Patrick and Sharon.

Buíochas le cairde agus gaolta: Máire Corry, Caoimhín Ó Comhraí, Gearóid Ó Tuathaigh, Dean Hanlon, Seán Ó Murchadha, Daithí Mac an Bhaird, Pádraig O'Reilly (Podge), Daithí Ó Madáin, Conor McNamara, Pádraig Óg Ó Ruairc (ach go háirithe, ní tharlódh an leabhar seo gan é), Antóin Mac Unfraidh, Ann, Cal, Albert, Lynn, Cian and Conor Muckley. Mo chuid tuismitheoirí agus deirfiúracha: Laoise, Orla, Caoimhe, Laoise agus Stiofán Ó Comhraí. Ar deireadh thiar thall míle buíochas le Sarah-Ann as ucht na tacaíochta a thug tú dom agus mé ag tabhairt faoi na tionscnaimh seo ar fad. Tá mé fíor-bhuíoch. Ar deireadh buíochas lenár mac Ben-Eoghan. Bodhróidh mé thú ag caint faoi na rudaí seo!

INDEX

E

F

G